Many are Cold but Few are Frozen

Plain tales from Antarctica

by
Graham Chambers

Strategic Book Publishing and Rights Co.

Strategic Book Publishing and Rights Co., LLC
USA I Singapore

For information about special discounts for bulk purchases,
please contact Strategic Book Publishing and Rights Co.
Special Sales, at bookorder@sbpra.net.

ISBN: 978-1-68181-425-4

Book Design: Suzanne Kelly

Introduction

The following stories are based on my stay as a meteorologist on the British Antarctic Survey (BAS) base of Halley Bay during 1974 and 1975.

Halley (as it is now called) is the most southerly of the BAS bases—being only some 500 miles from the South Pole.

The base complement was 18 males with a more-or-less 50/50 changeover of personnel after a year.

It was a unique experience and one with sights, sounds and smells which are not forgotten after forty years.

Each story is based on real events and essentially is a true recollection, barring a strictly limited amount of literary licence and the limitations of human recollection. It is worth mentioning in this respect the "witness" phenomenon, whereby 12 people can witness the very same event and produce at least half a dozen unique recollections of it.

Thanks are due to the characters who inadvertently animated the stories. Some names have been changed and others not.

Thanks are also due to the British Antarctic Survey, who gave me the wonderful opportunity to spend 2 years in the world's most exquisite destination.

Thanks too, to my wife Victoria and children, Malcolm and Penelope, who have had to put up with these and many other stories for longer than anyone should have to.

My experience after decades of recounting my experiences to audiences is that there are those who, while oohing and ahh-ing at photographs of Antarctica, would never want to go there, and those who immediately understand the attraction of Antarctica without even needing to see the pictures.

My message to the latter is to try by whatever means to visit Antarctica, and to leave it as you find it—pristine, unspoilt and immaculate.

CHAPTER ONE

Dr Tom.

Doctor Tom was a disaster waiting to happen. He often reflected that this was not a good thing for a doctor to be.

It's not that he wasn't competent—he was a more than adequate young doctor. Not only that, he reflected glumly, it wasn't even a question of competence.

He knew plenty of doctors who were less than competent, but who had—often in spades—the comforting appearance of being competent. They looked authoritative, genial and solid.

It's a sad truth that in this world appearances count for a lot. You can talk utter nonsense but with an appropriately authoritative air and dignified bearing people will swallow it like mothers' milk. Politicians thrive on this.

Tom was 25, a newly-qualified doctor aiming to go into general practice, but not before a little adventure.

Thus it was that he found himself being interviewed for a post as medical practitioner for the scientific base of Halley Bay, Antarctica for the 1973-4 season.

Halley was a geophysical base on the Coates Coast of the Weddell Sea. It was roughly 75 degrees South at about 500 miles from the South Pole and about 1 degree west, about the same longitude as Cornwall.

It didn't look like Cornwall, Tom reflected as the ice-strengthened ship *Bransfield* approached the brilliant white ice cliffs and the stretch of lower sea ice in what was known as "Second Chip".

Halley "floated" on an Ice Shelf about as large as Yorkshire connected to the inland ice of the Antarctic plateau about 60 miles south by an area of deep crevassing known as the Hinge Zone.

Thus the ice upon which Halley lay was not floating in the usual sense of the term, but underneath the 500 feet of ice was the sea.

The base itself was a collection of huts built inside tunnels made of very strong corrugated steel and connected by smaller tunnels of the same corrugated steel.

The whole complex was largely underneath the rapidly accumulating snow.

Indeed the rapid accumulation of the snow against any-thing which stood out on this vast, flat, windy plateau was the reason that the base was designed to be underground. Rather like a submarine, it lay beneath the snow with access to the outside via ladders in vertical shafts somewhat akin to conning towers.

First, Second and Third Chip were the prosaic names given to indentations in the ice-front about 5 miles from Halley itself.

These "chips" contained sea-ice of a decent thickness, even in the height of the Antarctic summer and were the places best suited for the annual "relief" when stores were unloaded.

Expedition members or Fids (from the old "Falkland Island Dependencies Survey") were also unloaded to spend a year or two on the base. They were often unloaded in the same way as the stores and so Tom's first contact with the Antarctic mainland was when he and about 10 others had to throw themselves into a large net spread on the hatchway and were then gathered up into a rabble by the tightening net as the crane lifted it, swung it over and lowered it onto the sea ice.

One of them didn't scramble inside quickly enough and so clung on to the outside and, shortly before the net was lowered, managed to fall off, hitting the soft snow with an almighty "thwack". It was, of course, Dr Tom.

Apart from glasses totally covered in snow and a severe shock, Dr Tom was unharmed and, as ever, completely unfazed by the incident, but there is no doubt that it added to his already considerable reputation.

Before arriving at Halley, the Bransfield had visited and relieved bases at South Georgia, Signy Island and Adelaide Island.

At Signy there was a 20-foot swell and stores for the base had to be loaded onto a barge known as the scow. Tom, also heading for the base, clung onto a rope net hung over the port side of the ship ready to jump into the scow as it came up on the swell- much further and faster of course than the 5000 tonne Bransfield.

Others jumped at the right moment and landed with an "Ouf!" onto the sacks of anthracite filling most of the scow. Tom jumped slightly later with the result that the scow was twelve feet lower against the net than it had been a split second before.

The "Ouf" was replaced in Tom's case by a sickening crunch as he spread-eagled onto the none-too comfortable sacks with considerable force, losing his glasses, without which he was blind as a bat, between the coal-dust covered sacks.

It wasn't that Dr Tom was gangly or awkward in the way that many teenagers appear to be—all arms and legs and poor co-ordination. He was short and exceedingly compact and with his curly and very dark red hair looked somewhat like a garden gnome. All in all he was not an unattractive young man, but he had always felt that a doctor should appear somehow more substantial, taller and with gravitas.

His clumsiness was perhaps also due to a distinct lack of circumspection, for Dr Tom was quite a physical extrovert.

In an unloading chain, for example, where heavy bags or boxes were passed from Fid to Fid, Dr Tom would tend to get carried away with sheer enthusiasm and chuck, rather than pass, the load to the next in the chain with the result that he was regularly cursed by the recipient.

It was in one of these chains that a Fid fell and seriously twisted his ankle and was in such pain that a break was suspected.

Dr Tom, at that time aboard ship, was immediately summoned and arrived at high speed a few minutes later complete with his classic doctors' Black Bag, in a "Gemini" rubber dinghy.

As the dinghy pulled in, Tom steadied himself and jumped onto the wooden-boarded jetty along which he ran full-pelt towards his putative patient.

Ignoring the unevenness of the boards, he tripped and went flying along the jetty while his black doctors' bag sailed into the air, over the jetty and landed in the sea, seriously frightening a group of seabirds, who had doubtless never had a doctors' bag thrown at them before.

It floated rather well for a while as onlookers watched transfixed by the scene, but then, slowly and with some dignity and grace, tilted as it filled with water, and softly disappeared beneath the dead-flat surface with an apologetic gurgle.

Apart from having again lost his glasses, Tom was not seriously hurt, although his limp as he rose and headed toward the patient suggested ankle trouble as well. The potential patient, having observed all this with a degree of horror, changed his mind about needing medical attention and was instead borne away to a bunk to recuperate naturally.

Dr Tom's bag was never seen again, but there were more than adequate medical supplies aboard ship and on all the scientific bases.

The job of base doctor, to be frank, was a bit of a sinecure.

Illness was rare. Fids were generally in their mental and physical prime and fitter in most cases than the general population.

Pests of the insect variety were unknown and in the case of micro-organisms, seriously compromised by the average temperatures which killed most before they had a chance to spread.

A minor series of snuffles often broke out among the wintering staff at the annual relief when the ship brought new germs with it, but these rarely lasted more than a few days.

The most likely cause of work for a base doctor was therefore accidents, usually minor and encountered while handling often heavy objects, such as 45-gallon oil drums, around the base. Thus the base doctor spent some of his time doing projects and using the base staff as guinea-pigs.

Thus other Fids were subjected to regular weighing, examinations, blood and urine samples, or whatever else was required to provide data for the particular project.

One thing that could be studied, at Halley in particular, was sleep patterns among those whose jobs did not involve fixed schedules.

Halley was pretty dark during the winter as the sun largely disappeared, appearing in Midwinter very briefly as a red glow on the horizon at about noon.

People such as diesel and garage mechanics, who could largely determine their own schedule of maintenance, often inverted their sleep patterns, working through the night and sleeping through the day.

In summer, there was a great temptation to stay up all night to enjoy the midnight sun and the long pale blue shadows which it cast across the ridged landscape, outlining the sharp profile of the sastrugi — ridges of hard snow formed by the wind.

Apart from such projects and the exciting possibility of having to perform an emergency appendectomy on the kitchentable in midwinter if weather conditions did not permit evacuation (a secret dream of many a doctor with romantic tendencies) boredom was the biggest risk for medical practitioners. They consequently tended to launch themselves into all manner of activities to keep themselves occupied.

There was a great deal of work to be done on a scientific base which was, once equipped and provisioned, essentially self-sufficient for a year.

Not only did regular "fuel-runs" have to be made to bring fuel from the fuel dump to the generator shed, but there was a regular "gash" run to take away garbage and trash.

In addition, there were regular water runs to bring fresh snow and load it into the melt tanks by shovelling it down the tubes which linked those tanks to the surface. No-one could take a shower without first filling up the melt tanks.

In addition there was always snow to be shifted from one place to another and the Halley Bay emblem included a pair of crossed shovels to emphasize this.

Thus Dr Tom, following tradition, became the principal bulldozer driver.

The bulldozers were in fact modified International Harvester tractors with a hydraulic blade attached. They were heavy, diesel-engine tracked beasts, though in Antarctica, since diesel freezes at only minus fifteen, it was replaced by aviation kerosene and the engine modified to allow for direct lubrication in the cylinders.

Around midwinter, when the temperature could remain in the minus 40's for weeks on end, a bulldozer was kept permanently with the engine running, since the difficulty of starting it, once stopped, was too great.

Although the tractor cabin had side doors, the roof was fitted with a hatch, the door of which had been removed since an incident some years previously when a newly-unloaded tractor had disappeared through the sea ice just metres away from the ship and the driver had to exit fast via the roof hatch. This made for a very cold cabin.

Once on base Dr Tom busied himself with fitting out his surgery — a room at the end of the dormitory block — and arranging the newly-arrived shipment of medicines, equipment and assorted paraphernalia which included an antediluvian X-ray machine of no doubt noble ancestry but dubious safety, and of which Dr Tom was inordinately proud.

His somewhat boisterous nature was soon apparent to all his new colleagues on base as well as those who had known him on board ship.

The base complement was 18 and of this 10 were new and eight had already spent a year at Halley.

The floors of the base huts being surfaced with a kind of modern linoleum, the corridors were perfect for base members to skate on while wearing the thick woollen socks which were standard interior footwear.

Dr Tom quickly took to this mode of transport as the fastest means of getting from one end of a block to the other. It was unfortunate that he reached the open door at the end of the dorm block intending to pass into the connecting tunnel when someone, not hearing or seeing him, shut the heavy door, with which Dr Tom collided with considerable momentum.

Although Dr Tom was a popular, enthusiastic and hardworking member of the team one could sense and indeed understand the certain reluctance on the part of his companions to take part in his experiments—or even to fall ill or report to the surgery with a minor wound.

Base routine was rigid. Saturday evening was a fairly formal dinner, some even going to the trouble of dressing in dinner-jacket for special occasions such as birthdays or Midwinter.

Sunday was "scrub-out" day and in the morning all except the sleeping night shift would join in with the polishing, sweeping and scrubbing of the entire building.

Once this was done a Sunday brunch of cold cuts, cheeses, sandwiches and delicacies of various kinds was organised in the lounge, thus giving the cook a rest.

There followed a lazy afternoon of reading, listening to music or to old BBC records illegally obtained via the Falklands of such ancient and classic programmes as "Take it from here", "Round the Horne", "I'm sorry I'll read that again", "The Navy Lark" and "The Goon Show".

It was while listening to one of these that someone remarked that he hadn't seen Dr Tom all day. Others concurred and before long we ascertained that no-one had seen him at all that Sunday.

It was about 3 in the afternoon by this time and the outside weather was calm and clear though being early spring, very cold at around minus 35 Centigrade.

Once it had been determined that he was neither in his surgery, his bed, nor the toilet, a search of the base from end to end was organized, checking the garage, the diesel generator room, the hobby room, the geophysics and met rooms and even the attic, where amongst many other things, the porn magazines were stored.

No trace having been found and some degree of concern being manifest someone checked out the darkroom—a much used facility—and then an outside search was organised taking in the "Beastie hut" (the Beastie being a particularly complex piece of transmitter/receiver gear for analysing the Ionosphere), the geophysics tunnel, the meteorological radar and the general surroundings of the base.

By this time, the base members were using aluminium poles to penetrate the soft snow in case he had fallen or become ill and been covered by the slightly blowing snow.

It was the electrician who noticed that one of the IH bull-dozers was standing way over at the fuel dump, where a couple of 45 gallon drums served as the filling-station. The horizontal plume of exhaust swiftly descending in the very cold air told us its engine was running.

Affixed to the rear of each tractor cabin about 1.5 metres from the ground was a hand-operated pump comprising a cast pump housing with a half-metre wooden handle pointing verti-cally upward and two rubber hoses attached to the inlet and outlet valves.

The outlet hose led to the tractor's fuel tank, the inlet hose was inserted by the driver into a 45 gallon drum and rapid side to side movement of the pump handle resulted in fuel being transferred from the drum into the tank.

A group of Fids approached the tractor but could see no sign of Dr Tom, until one of the group went round the back of the tractor and exploded into fits of laughter.

"Quick—go and get a camera, and hurry." he said—rather inhumanely under the circumstances because there was Tom, hanging by his anorak on the vertical pump handle and utterly immobile.

His glasses had completely frozen over and he was as still as death. After the shock of the sight, pandemonium broke out with everyone at once trying to lift the thoroughly stiff body off the pump handle.

His anorak and windproof trousers were as stiff as a hospital matron's apron and his rigid body was carried horizontally on the shoulders of 4 men as quickly as possible into the warmth of the base and straight through into the surgery.

It was at first impossible to remove either his anorak or his windproof over-trousers, so wooden had they become and so an additional heater was brought in and he was wrapped in blankets.

A heartbeat was detected and after about half an hour some movement of both clothing and Dr. Tom. Further detail is unnecessary. Suffice to say that within a couple of hours he was awake, though drowsy, in bed and was taking as much hot soup as the cook could get into him.

From his bed he told the nursing team what to give him in the way of medication and after a full night's sleep under supervision he was pretty much back to normal the following day.

He was damned lucky to have been found when he was. He had decided to go out for a bit of bulldozing that morning and, with a near empty fuel tank, had driven to the "filling station".

As mentioned earlier the IH tractors had a roof opening and it had become the practice to leave the side doors shut to keep out wind and snow and to enter and exit the cabin by the hatch.

Dr. Tom, with typical enthusiasm, had stood on the seat, pulled himself out of the roof hatch and slid down the back of the cabin to refuel—only to discover to his immense frustration that the vertical pump handle had slipped between him and his anorak and lodged firmly in the collar, leaving him dangling helplessly with his short frame about a metre from the ground.

Much agitation had ensued, thrashing left and right, trying to get out of his anorak, trying to find something, anything, on the smooth back of the tractor cabin on which he could place his feet—all without success.

Shouting was hopeless. The exertion had clouded his glasses which then froze so that he could no longer see. Nor could he remove his glasses, and gradually his movement ceased as he tried to conserve what little body heat remained.

Though the incident could have been tragic and was undoubtedly for Tom seriously traumatic, he soon recovered and regained his old self, once more skating in socks at full speed along the linoleum corridors.

Some months later, when someone on base had an accident in which they fell into a mantrap crevasse and twisted a foot, no-one was in the least surprised to discover that it was Dr Tom.

CHAPTER TWO

Bat out of hell.

Ian the diesel mechanic was sure he knew where it was. So was Gordon the tractor mech. Trouble was they didn't agree.

We all knew roughly what it looked like, since there were some photographs of it around. It dated back to the International Geophysical Year and there were tales of it being used by Sir Vivian Fuchs.

No-one was quite sure of its name, but it was known by some as the Faireyplane. This, you understand, had nothing to do with ethereal creatures found at the bottom of the garden, but with the Fairey Aviation Company—a British maker of aeroplanes of the 1950's.

One thing was sure. It was buried under possibly 2-3 metres of snow somewhere out on the Bundu near to Halley II.

It was obviously completely buried. Given the length of time it had been there and its size, it must be completely covered. Certainly nothing had been seen despite frequent searches in places where various people thought it might be.

There were, however certain parameters which helped to determine its general location. It was pretty certain that it was east of the base and indeed somewhat north of east. It was certainly within 200 metres and it was possibly along a line running approximately NW-SE where it had been customary to park various old vehicles of dubious use and provenance.

Amongst these were the "Elsan" (or Eliason motor tobog-gan—a splendid 1950s relic) and the wonderful Bog Rol (sic) invented by Ian Bury, a cook on Halley II with a remarkable capacity for eccentricity. The Bog Rol had somewhat miraculously, given its small size, been found and so had the "Elsan", though at least a year previously.

The "Elsan" indeed was operative due entirely to the fact that it was powered by a 4-stroke Briggs and Stratton lawn-mower engine, which, after refuelling and light brushing around the plug and coil, had started first time and since then was characterised by the difficulty in stopping it.

It was almost certainly the tip of the aluminium propeller which was first seen and which identified the location of the "Plane". Perhaps there had been a long "blow" and much of the sastrugi surface had been eroded. Perhaps someone tripped over it or ski-jored over it. Whatever the reason, digging around the protuberance proved that it was indeed a blade of the prop and that all that remained was to carefully dig out the rest of the machine.

This had to be done carefully because the machine itself was lightly built of aluminium sheets, riveted together to form a pear-shaped cabin with two seats side by side, mounted on a set of skids, the front parts of which were moveable and attached to a steering wheel in the cabin.

The rear of the machine comprised the immoveable part of the skids and a platform onto which was fixed a frame of aluminium tubing and this in turn supported a 4 cylinder petrol engine at the front of which the propeller was attached.

Being on night duty the week in which it was found meant that I took no part in the digging which was accomplished by Andy, Richard, Ian and John. Ian, the diesel mechanic, was something of a night owl since he preferred to see to his generators in peace during the night. He was a Scot who appeared at first to be of taciturn mien, but in fact was a very likeable and eccentric individual with a great sense of humour and the absurd, which is absolutely necessary in the Antarctic. He also shortened his name to "Ee."

Although the diesel mech was principally responsible for the generators, Ee was also a great help to the tractor mechanic and once re-jigged a Muskeg tractor which had terminal failure in one cylinder by turning it from a 6 cylinder engine into a

5-cylinder engine (something of a feat considering the re-timing and cam adjustment and other magical measures needed). The resultant "flying five" worked rather well. So "Ee" it was who cleaned and reassembled the engine of the plane.

And the bugger worked! With a roar the thing came to life. There must have been some sort of clutch, or the thing would have shot off across the bundu there and then and it would have been quite impossible to catch it. There was certainly no brake (how could there be apart from a drag parachute and we didn't have one of those). We did however have an anchor (or grappling hook) and this with a length of rope tied to one of the skis became the emergency brake!

Maybe we drew straws for driving the thing, but I think that the mechanics were the first to have this dubious honour. It was spring and the temperatures were still between 20 and 30 below and the bundu was hard as concrete.

The cabin seats were not comfortable and even if they had been the utter lack of decent suspension would still have meant a very uncomfortable ride.

The thing shot off and it was quickly discovered that its turning circle was about a kilometre and in addition, it was soon lost in a cloud of spindrift which the propeller kicked-up from the surface.

In the following days and weeks, various people took it out for a spin. Those who did not want to sit inside it discovered that you could ski-jore behind it on the end of a rope and increase your speed considerably by swinging from side to side.

The downside of this was that it was practically impossible to see where you were going because of the utter lack of visibility in the spindrift.

On second thoughts maybe this was an advantage at that speed and over those knee-smashing sastrugi. When you finally stopped you were completely caked with hard snow almost from head to foot.

As spring progressed we had days with much sunshine and the surface started to soften, which made the going easier, but the spindrift worse. At Halley on fine days with high pressure there was often a quite considerable temperature inversion. This could be experienced personally by the simple expedient of climbing the meteorological tower which was done sometimes to take care of the anemometer.

While the surface temperature could be minus 30, the temperature at the top of the tower (only 10 metres) could be 15 degrees higher.

The inversion could be clearly seen on the temperature chart resulting from the daily balloon flight where in calm conditions the temperature trace would swing violently to the right (warmer) almost immediately the sonde had left terra-firma. With a surface wind the effect was less immediate, but still apparent.

One particular day the weather was exceptionally fine — pure "dingle" as the term went, with cerulean skies, miraged icebergs on the horizon and absolutely no wind.

In such conditions with a steep temperature inversion, strange optical phenomena were observed. Icebergs, detached from the shelf and floating or grounded many kilometres offshore were "refracted up" and seen perfectly well as though much nearer.

Sometimes they were inverted and even double inverted -what you saw was the upright refraction of the iceberg with an upside-down image on top of it.

Such conditions seemed ideal for a trip out to the "coast", but were in fact quite deadly. The coast consisted of cliffs with indentations locally known as "chips", but in these conditions you could simply not be sure of seeing what was really there and ran the risk of heading for a non-existent promontory and falling over the cliff as a result.

All along the Coates Coast and in the whole of the Weddell Sea area that day scientific stations—the Argentineans at Belgrano, the South Africans at SANAE and the Russians at Druzhnaya all recorded clear blue sky and perfect visibility.

All except Halley, for mid morning someone had been out for a jolly in the Plane. Round and round the base they had gone, in as tight a turning circle as they could manage and wherever they went the Plane's propeller thoroughly mixed the stagnant air from the surface to about 10 metres above it.

Fog can be caused by various processes. It is most usually very low cloud in mountains actually coming into contact with the ground. Elsewhere it can occur when warm wet air meets colder air or land and the resultant cooling and condensation creates the fine water droplets or ice particles which make up fog. In cities of course it can be caused or at least exacerbated by pollution.

At Halley none of these was the case. Advective fog is formed when air of differing temperatures and humidities is mixed by either natural or unnatural means.

Not half an hour after the circling of the base by the Plane, Halley was obscured totally by thick ice-fog leading to a visibility of less than 50 metres. The meteorological observations as a result thereafter showed fog for the rest of the day, the only place in an area the size of Western Europe where the weather was not perfect, pristine, blue-sky and sunshine.

The exact date of the incident was not recorded, but if the meteorological records for spring 1974 were carefully analysed for the southern Weddell Sea, the anomaly would pinpoint the date quite precisely.

CHAPTER THREE

Going to the dogs.

Muff was as thick as two short planks, but cute—you couldn't help but like him.

Innocent as a newborn, furry, big-hearted, daft as a brush and awfully, awfully keen. Tail wagging furiously, eyes bright, tongue lolling out between his teeth—he was obviously pleased to see you. Whether it was food, or a run or just a quick cuddle hello as you passed by, Muff was in for them all.

His brother Brae was quite, quite, different.

Perhaps his name said it all for there was something of the Scottish dourness about Brae. A certain lack of enthusiasm, a lack of abandon, a certain careful calculation about the dog. He was no doubt intelligent—highly so and much more than his brother, but it was a cold, calculating intelligence. Even his love, of which he would give a little in exchange for food and warmth, seemed to be weighed and doled out in quanta, never amounting to more than he got in return.

The two dogs were physically very different. Muff resembled a small bear or perhaps a panda, though obviously not only black and white. He was fluffy and his head was large.

If Muff was ursine, Brae was very definitely vulpine. His head was smaller and not so much wider than his neck. He had less fur on him and his neck at the top appeared as if it had been back-combed permanently, giving him a kind of unkempt ruff. He was smaller overall than Muff and may well have emerged as the last of the litter—the runt.

The first time I had been asked to feed the two dogs, they were out on the "spans". These were lengths of thin steel cable stretched on the ground between two pegs in parallel. Each dog was attached to the "span" by a lead and so could run up and down the span, giving them the ability to exercise without total freedom. Given that, they would have run off and either got lost or got down to the sea-ice in winter and met seals or penguins, with predictable results.

They were fed a kind of dried pemmican-like bar which we called "nutty" (this was also what we called chocolate, whether or not it contained nuts).

The odd thing about chocolate is that, for some people at least, it tastes so much better when very cold. Ours usually was very cold—freezing, in fact and there were those who got used to this and liked it. Even inside the base, people put a bar of chocolate in the ice cave for at least an hour before eating a piece. Whether Muff and Brae preferred their "nutty" freezing cold there is no way of knowing, for they never had it any other way.

As well as "nutty", they had to have some real meat and so the base was allowed to kill a couple of seal each year which were then cut up and the meat stored in our food-cave hollowed out of the ice which kept everything at a steady minus 20.

In addition, we gave the dogs the occasional treat of butter.

Our sledging rations had been determined in the heroic days of sledging expeditions, either with dogs or man-hauling and the butter allowance per man per week was amazing. The butter was from New Zealand and came in 1 pound cans. The ration was something close to a pound per man per day!

There was plenty of butter and so the duty gash-man was asked to give the dogs a can each as well as their "nutty". He went to the kitchen and dutifully opened the can with the heavy-duty opener when Colin the dog-man, saw what he was doing. "Don't do that" he said. Puzzled, the gash man asked what he was supposed to do. "Just chuck the cans at 'em" was the reply.

Indeed, that was the only thing one needed to do. They seemed to enjoy crushing the cans with their powerful jaws and making a game out of getting all the butter from within. After they had finished, the can did not remotely resemble what it had once been. Since they were used to eating meat frozen solid at minus 30 to 40, it was obvious when you thought about it that a tin can posed no problem at all for them.

There had been a time, in the heroic age, when Halley had a complement of 60 or more dogs and dog teams drew sleds all over the interior ice-sheet and rugged explorer types mapped and triangulated. They calculated their latitude and longitude from star observations and their trajectory from compass readings and distance travelled.

This was recorded using the little gizmo which people used to attach to their bicycle forks and which used to count every time the little screw attached to one of the wheel spokes knocked against the little star on the counter, thus counting the rotations of the wheel.

We lived in less heroic times when the dogs had gone- apart from two, who were kept for company and, one suspects, old times' sake. Muff and Brae were our pets and much loved.

The dogs were regularly taken out for runs. They were attached (in parallel, rather than in series, to use an electrical image), by lamp-wick harnesses to a rope which was in turn attached to a belt which was worn around the waist of the human who was then pulled on a pair of cross-country skis, rather different to the sleek and slim-line models of today.

These skis were as wide as alpine skis and had a metal front binding which held a regular boot—the ones we referred to as RBLTs (for rubber bottom/leather top). A wire coiled cable went around the back of the boot enabling the wearer to lift the back of the boot from the ski while still remaining attached.

With a bit of encouragement the dogs set off and could, in good conditions, get up to a fair speed, although the speed always increased on the way back to the spans and food! Turning was effected by shouting the commands "Irrrrr" for right and "Auk" for left. Some people always had trouble with this, for the "Irrrrr" had to be pronounced with a rolled "r" or a Scots burr.

Being short-tongued, some found this very hard to do and it always came out as "Iwwww". The dogs did not understand this at all. As a result dog drivers with this mild speech impediment tended to go in an anticlockwise circle so that they could get away with just using "Auk".

The time came for two of us to take the dogs and a sled and go travelling -just a short break. We decided on the Low Shelf.

The topography of Halley and its surroundings was not unlike that of the Fens—flat with huge skies, but not a lot of distinguishing landmarks on the ground. There were really only a couple of worthwhile destinations.

There was the "Hinge Zone" inland, where the ice shelf left its bed of underlying rock and started to float and which, as a result of the unending, if slight, movement was highly crevassed.

There was the Emperor penguin colony, but this was deemed rather too close to the base to count as an expedition destination and so there was only one destination left—the Low Shelf.

The thing that distinguished the Low Shelf was that it was part of the main ice-shelf, but it was low as its name might suggest and the ice cliffs were much more amenable to descent onto the sea-ice and in parts there were no cliffs at all. We decided on the Low Shelf.

The Nansen sledge was prepared and packed with radio box, ration box and primus box and the tent was strapped over the lot. Total weight about 380 kilos. The two dogs could pull that, but there was no question of either Ken or I hanging onto the sled. We skied alongside.

To the back of the sled was attached our distance reckoner, namely the front fork of a bicycle with the wheel. Attached to the fork was the aforementioned gizmo—a small hexagonal counter which, in theory, clicked every time the wheel turned and the small contact on the spokes hit the star shaped wheel of the counter. This was converted into kilometres.

Unfortunately, this seemingly serendipitous arrangement had one fatal flaw... after some hours travelling we discovered that the star-shaped wheel regularly failed to turn when hit (or rather missed) by the contact on the spokes.

Navigation was by dead reckoning, a compass giving the direction and the bicycle wheel counter the distance travelled.

Alas, the counter gave us nothing of the kind so that although we knew in which direction we had travelled, we had no accurate idea of how far we had gone in that direction.

This may seem to be a critical flaw, but in fact precise navigation is only necessary where there is somewhere definite to head for and obstacles or places to either avoid or visit on the way.

The Bundu around Halley was largely free of either of these, consisting as it did of seemingly endless flat white nothingness. Not to get too philosophical about it, but navigating one's way across nothingness really doesn't present too many problems.

The Low Shelf is not a precise place, but a considerable length of coastline.

We knew where the sea was because of the Halley summer phenomenon of clear sky over the ice shelf and stratocumulus cloud over the sea, a thick layer of cloud which reflected the dark, open, unfrozen summer ocean.

Our task was consequently simple—to follow the coast without getting too near (thus avoiding indentations in the coast or "chips"), because they tended to conceal crevasses. Refraction due to temperature inversion also made the coast treacherous—what we saw was apparent, rather than real.

Consequently the non-operative bicycle wheel counter was an amusing diversion, rather than a serious problem. We decided to ignore it.

We had not been travelling for more than 3 hours, at a steady pace when we both noticed something rather odd. Stopping as we did frequently for a breather, we noticed that Muff was puffing like a steam engine and panting furiously, tongue lolling out of his mouth and his breath freezing in the very cold, dry air, whereas Brae was hardly panting at all.

A little more observation from Ken, who skied ahead, confirmed what we had begun to suspect. Brae was simply moving enough to keep his harness tight, but was contributing practically nothing to the effort of pulling the sled. The motive power was supplied almost entirely by Muff.

Another dog, less good-natured and, dare one say, less dim, might have given Brae a damn good bite.

19

It soon became clear on further observing the two dogs that Muff was not bothered about Brae's lack of effort—not because he was a forgiving and loving animal, which he undoubtedly was, but because he quite simply had not noticed. But what could we do about it?

As far as we knew (and of course the days of the "Doggy men"—experts in getting huskies to work- were long past) you had two choices—a "fan" trace in which 9 or more dogs were attached in fan fashion to the sled, with the lead dog slightly ahead, or a long single trace with two dogs attached at intervals and the lead dog in front.

With only two dogs, there were two possibilities, to harness them either "in parallel" or "in series"—together, or one behind the other.

We had been using the first option of both dogs together.

Would the alternative be any better? If Muff were in front, Brae could still pull only as much as needed to keep the trace taut. If Brae were in front and Muff as usual pulling as hard as he could, Brae would have difficulty in calculating how hard to pull to keep the trace taut and so could more easily be caught out.

We decided that Brae would lead the following day.

Meantime, there was camp to pitch and the evening meal to prepare.

It was very cold. As we drew to a halt on a piece of Bundu as unprepossessing as the rest and untied the tent and equipment from the sledge, our freezing breath and the feel of contact through our mitts told us that the temperature was already in the low minus twenties.

Ken set the dogs out on the span and threw some nutty at them. We had already put up the tent and I was busy furnishing it by blowing up two li-los, covering each with a luxurious sheepskin and laying out our sleeping bags- each one with a canvas outer cover, an outer down-filled bag and within that an inner down-filled bag. Between the "beds" went the ration box and the primus box.

Morning dawned bright, cold and clear. It was minus 35 on base according to the radio operator when we called in for the morning "sched", so it must have been at least as cold where we were. It felt colder, although there was no wind and so it was not in the least unpleasant.

I was outside wearing only pyjamas and sheepskin tent boots and cleaning my teeth while scanning the horizon.

My scan came to a quick halt when I noticed something on the horizon which should not have been there. It was Brae, off his span and just lurking within frustration distance. Close enough to be seen and recognised, but nowhere near close enough to be caught. I motioned to Ken, who had already seen him. Any motion we made was immediately followed by a movement further away by Brae. It was infuriating. We could hardly let him trot along at a suitably safe distance with Muff alone doing the pulling.

He had slipped his harness rather easily. Given his thin neck and small head, it was not difficult for him to extend his neck and slowly back out of the harness, which had previously been tight.

He obviously wasn't hungry, since Ken's ferreting out a bar of nutty with great ceremony seemed to interest him not at all. He kept looking at us, but would run back and forth, always keeping a safe distance and occasionally lying down to watch us in comfort.

We packed everything up in the hope that Brae would be encouraged, or shamed, into returning, though if he didn't we couldn't go very far with Muff pulling by himself.

We harnessed Muff, compliant and eager as ever and held up the trace for Brae to see and hopefully wish to emulate, but no reaction at all apart from academic interest seemed to come from him. I could almost believe there was a self-satisfied grin on his face.

There was nothing for it but to get going with Muff pulling and Ken and I pushing in the hope that Brae, who at least seemed to know where his next meal was most likely to come from, would tag along.

Tag along he did, just far enough away to avoid a sudden lunge by either Ken or myself to grab him yet close enough to cause Muff to veer towards his brother constantly, apparently for a friendly sniff—in Muff's place I would have bitten him!

It was hard enough keeping the sledge going in a straight line and pushing the thing entailed going without skis, which were tied to the sledge. Going without skis meant increased danger of falling into an invisible crevasse and the attention needed to keep the sledge straight, keep Muff from going anywhere but straight ahead and keeping an eye on Brae was wearing in the extreme.

Finally the inevitable occurred. Muff backtracked as Brae stayed behind to pee and the sledge turned on its side, throwing me over flat onto the bundu. Ken seized the moment of confusion and managed to grab Brae hard by the collar and hold on. Caught!

The lamp-wick collar was put back on, but this time, while Brae was held, the sledge was righted and unpacked and a spare harness found. There was nothing for it but to do something quite unconventional—namely put the second harness over Brae's rear end, inserting his back legs into the holes and attaching the two harnesses together.

This way, however ridiculous he looked (and he did) and however uncomfortable it was (and we did have sympathy for his undercarriage), there was no way he could wriggle out of his harness by squeezing his head out, since the rear harness was still attached to the front one and to wriggle out of the rear harness was beyond him.

Safely attached to the trace, Brae looked miserable and put upon. Once on the move again, it was difficult to tell whether Brae was contributing anything to the efforts of Muff or simply going at a pace sufficient to keep the trace looking tight.

Since after some time, Muff was not totally exhausted; we concluded that Brae was contributing something to the effort, but probably not much.

The Low Shelf was reached. The open water was clearly delineated in the sky by the reflection of the dark open water on the blanket of stratocumulus cloud.

We spanned the dogs—very carefully in the case of Brae and fed them. The tent was erected and the inside made comfortable, not to say cosy once the primus was lit and food prepared.

As a special celebration we ate a starter of oxtail soup with a big lump of butter dissolved in it as well as the contents of a tin of sardines in oil, (the taste combination was irrelevant—what we needed was fat—candle wax would have done).

This was followed by pemmican bar dissolved in melted snow with added curry powder, dried onions and more butter. We then flambéed peaches in brandy (almost setting the tent alight in the process) and opened a tin of frozen Carnation milk, which served as ice-cream. A feast fit for a king!

During the night both of us heard the sound of very heavy breathing. Having ascertained that neither of us was responsible, we remained puzzled until, in the morning, while padding around outside in mukluks and pyjamas we both noticed some 50 metres away at the edge of the low shelf, rhythmically rising plumes of what appeared to be steam.

Quickly dressing, we headed onto the low shelf ice and carefully moved towards its sea-edge, watching carefully for any sign of cracks. The shelf appeared very solid and so we carefully approached the source of the noise, which was now very loud, and the "steam".

What we saw made us both jump with excitement for, heads against or even slightly upon the ice edge were four great whales with big hairy mouths behind which were relatively small eyes, breathing rhythmically from their blowholes. We reckoned them to be 10 to 15 metres or so in length and possibly Fin or Sei whales. Fin whales are the world's biggest after the rare Blue whale. The sight was quite spectacular and we were close enough to reach out and touch their snouts, though caution prevented us from doing so.

It is hardly likely they would have noticed, but we were all-too aware that if they took exception and moved suddenly, they were quite capable of cracking the ice. We retreated slowly, immensely grateful for having seen what we had. The Low

Shelf as a destination in itself is nothing spectacular, but this had made the trip more than worthwhile.

It was time to return. Camp was struck, the sledge loaded and the dogs hitched up to it. There was no trouble from Brae at all and as we set off, he seemed eager to pull as hard as possible. Of course the answer to this change of heart was obvious—he knew we were heading home and nothing would stop him from pulling as hard as he could to get there.

CHAPTER FOUR

The life of Bryan.

Bryan did not leave many people neutral; indeed he could be described as a natural polarizer. The base divided into those who couldn't stand him, those who idolized him (a minority), those who, because of the independent nature of their work or their character, managed to ignore him, and those who, working independently or at night, contrived to avoid him almost entirely.

Bryan was the Base-Commander, a post which, legally, made him the magistrate for an area as big as France, but with a total population of 18. He was a GA, or general assistant and originally a builder from Liverpool.

He was capable and competent in his field, but had a naturally argumentative, not to say combative character. He seemed to suffer from a kind of inverted snobbery and his undoubted talents were somewhat overshadowed by his constant insistence that he knew everything about everything.

He enjoyed arguing about anything at all and a regular protagonist was Chris, a Scots geophysicist of Polish origin and a man not likely to let a remark go uncontested. Thus in the bar, on a regular basis, we would be treated to a right ding-dong between these two on any subject under the sun.

Bryan was also a Mormon, although to his credit, he never tried to convert anyone else. No, his problem was simply that he was bigheaded.

That wasn't all. A Base-Commander has a tough job. Although Fids were screened to some extent to weed out those with too extrovert a temperament, or at least to ensure that not too many extroverts were put together, Bryan was undoubtedly an extrovert and, unfortunately for a Base-Commander, no diplomat.

Were oil to be poured on troubled waters, he could be relied upon to set fire to it. On a base such as Halley, with more than its fair share of prima donnas among its university scientists, this was not ideal.

Bryan had not been to university and all too obviously felt this keenly, hence his regular insistence (not entirely unfounded) that people who had been to university were not necessarily more intelligent that the rest, and that there was nothing to compete with the "university of life".

Bryan had indeed seen and done a lot. On a static, scientific base such as Halley, he was unique in having traversed large areas of the Antarctic Peninsular using dog sled from the legendary centre of rugged exploration in the old style—Stonington base.

He knew a lot about sledging, climbing, descending into crevasses and the sort of thing that for us at Halley, was romantic, impressive, but largely superfluous.

Bryan made, or rather had others make a wonderful job of reorganising the sledging equipment, turning a room into a miraculously ordered series of shelves and bins, painted in bright red, on or in which were stacked and stored airbeds, sheepskins, primus stoves, inner and outer tents, sledging boxes, field radios, sledging rations, crampons, harnesses, lamp- wick, sledging gloves and all the assorted paraphernalia which accompanied rugged exploration activities. All of it was catalogued and classified in wondrous order and listed in a book which hung on a hook at the entrance of the store.

The base was new—Halley 3—and since early 1973 had replaced Halley 2, which was deep under the ice and in the process of being crushed slowly by the weight of ice above and around it. The new base was a new design, a series of light wooden huts built inside flattened spheroidal tunnels made of Armco—a very strong zinc-electroplated corrugated steel used in civil engineering constructions.

A vast amount of equipment had had to be moved from the old base to the new and this meant a considerable amount of work needed to be done in the new base to fit-out and finish and order and store everything. Head Office had perhaps decided that it needed a bit of a bulldozer in charge in this first year and in Bryan they had found their man.

One thing in particular needled some people — Bryan was not someone who led from the front, but someone who gave out orders and then tended to remain in his office with charts and diagrams and rather daft (mainly American) books about how to organize people, how to run companies, organizations and suchlike.

The door to his office was usually closed and the temperature within was a stifling 26 degrees.

Outside, the daily corvee would dig out snow from the garage ramp, do a fuel run or lay out lines of empty fuel drums to help navigate around the base. There were also many lines made from dunnage (planks used to separate cargo in a ship's hold) linked with sisal cord or in many cases, carrying cables to the outer huts and instruments.

There were two schools of thought about cables. One said they should be laid on the ground and left to be covered by the snow, the other that they should be held up by dunnage cut at the top with a "V" notch and regularly raised.

The first philosophy claimed that, once buried, the cables would be immune from vibration and stress and hence trouble-free.

The second philosophy held that cable was never trouble-free and that when a fault occurred, it could be found and rectified only if the cables were above ground. There was no resolution to this clash of philosophies, but it was true that cables supported on dunnage also served as lifelines to aid in navigation during blizzards.

Lifelines they literally were. In a severe "blow", the temperature could rise 20 degrees in four hours and the blowing snow become so thick and soft that you could not see your own hand if held out at arm's length.

In conditions such as this, all perspective was lost and a black object could just as easily be a matchbox a metre away or a tractor half a kilometre away. There was no way of telling distance, proportion or orientation.

One of the daily tasks on base was the launching of a weather balloon by the meteorologists. The soft latex balloon was filled with hydrogen and released with a radar reflector and a sonde attached.

The sonde was a light, disposable, battery-powered instrument, which gave continuous readings of temperature, pressure and humidity and converted these into morse code which was then transmitted as the sonde went up through the atmosphere until the balloon burst, usually at about 40,000 feet. The resulting data gave a profile of the atmosphere. In addition, the balloon was tracked by radar to enable its course to be plotted.

The radar was a white cabin atop a flat three-legged framework set up and levelled on the snow surface some distance from the base. Attached to the front was a radar dish in blue painted steel and at each side of the cabin was a door. Inside were two seats.

The left hand seat was for the driver and the right-hand one for the plotter.

For the morning flight, the duty balloon man would produce the hydrogen, fill the balloon and launch it with the sonde and radar reflector attached on a long line.

In the base met office, the receiver would emit the morse code and the "ditter" would sit with headphones on and transcribe the figures transmitted in Morse onto a special graph as the "flight" proceeded. In the meantime, the radar crew would follow the course of the balloon.

Piloting the radar was a specialist job requiring a certain knack or talent. The radar dish could be moved up to about 90 degrees or down to about 0 degrees and the whole cabin could be swung, like a tank turret, in a circle. The driver sat with a cathode-ray tube facing him and between his knees a steering device comprising a column on the end of which were two 6 inch plastic wheels set parallel to the driver's legs.

Each wheel had a rotating plastic knob on its circumference to enable it to be turned faster. The left hand wheel elevated or depressed the radar dish when rotated toward or away from the driver. The right hand wheel moved the cabin to the right when rotated toward the driver and to the left when rotated away.

The cathode ray tube showed an orange circle when the dish was pointed directly at the radar reflector attached to the balloon. When the balloon moved to the right, the left hand side of the circle would fade. When the balloon moved up, the bottom of the circle would fade. The idea was to keep a full circle in view on the screen.

It does not take much imagination to realize that piloting the radar needed a special knack, not unlike that of patting one's head and rubbing one's stomach in a circular motion at the same time. Not everyone can do it well.

Bryan, from the beginning, had wanted to pilot the radar, and after a few tries, had proved himself very competent. However, this hardly justified his boasting, which gave the impression that he was the Von Richthofen of the radar squadron.

One Sunday in autumn the temperature during the night had shot up from minus 32 to about minus 13 degrees in 5 hours and the wind speed from zero to nearly 40 knots.

In the morning light, hardly anything could be seen and the duty met man had made his way along the dunnage line to the Stevenson Screen to read the thermometers, barometer and hygrometer and clean out the accumulated drift from the inside. He was helped along the line by the screaming wind, against which he had to fight to return to the base.

That morning I was the wind plotter and Bryan had elected to pilot the radar.

We both made our way along the dunnage line which led to the radar. Bryan entered the left hand and I the right hand door and both silently made our preparations.

In such difficult weather conditions, piloting the radar was easy. The balloon, once launched, would move fast but in a straight line and given the strain to which it was subject, would tend to burst early before it got high enough to escape the wind and start to move in mysterious ways. This was the case that day and we got on with our jobs with hardly a word spoken between us.

As soon as Bryan announced "balloon burst", I took my plot and exited the cabin, holding onto the sisal line for life in extremely bad visibility.

Once back in the base, I was occupied in plotting the winds and then in taking the whole balloon flight data to the radio shack for transmission. It was usual for the radar pilot to stay longer in order to shut down the radar, bring the dish down and align it downwind and put on the parking brake. After that, Bryan would have returned to the BC's office.

By lunchtime, most of the base personnel were gathering in the lounge where a Sunday brunch was served. No-one had seen Bryan and a check in the BC's office, next to the lounge, found it empty. Lunch continued, followed by some old records of radio programmes, as was usual on Sunday, which was also the day on which the base was thoroughly scrubbed out in the morning. No doubt Bryan was checking something somewhere.

By 4 o'clock, there was still no sign of him and various people who had been out to surrounding huts to take measurements reported no sighting of Bryan. A certain anxiety mingled with curiosity had begun to take hold.

I was asked on more than one occasion to recount what had happened that morning during the balloon flight and recalled that, when I had left the radar to return to the base, Bryan was still in the radar, closing it down. The weather had worsened and visibility was so low that I had clung to the sisal line all the way back to the base entrance.

By this time, it was darkening and a full search was made of the interior of the base. People went out to the various huts where he might be, including of course, the radar, which had been shut down and showed no sign of anything abnormal.

Later that evening, the radio operator sent a message to BAS HQ informing them that the BC had gone missing. We all went to bed in very serious mood. Like him or loath him, everyone was disturbed at this strange turn of events.

Early next morning teams were organized to walk across the base area, tied together with rope and using aluminium poles to probe the soft, drifting snow in case he had fallen, become ill and lay covered under the snow.

First the route from the base to the radar was gone over and over again, then the base area was combed starting from the immediate surroundings and moving out in a grid pattern marked by flags.

Visibility was only slightly better, but the temperature was dropping and the wind also, leading to that most dangerous combination of 20/20 (minus 20 degrees and 20 knots of wind) resulting in a very high wind-chill factor.

We could only hope that, if he were alive, he had managed to dig in somewhere in the lee of an object and keep warm enough to stay awake. — Here there was some optimism. Bryan was experienced in the field and would instinctively know what to do. He was wearing a favourite coat from the air-force with high insulation qualities and a very good fur-trimmed hood. He was wearing very thick sledging gloves known as "bear paws", which he had been given by the Americans (they were not standard BAS issue).

In addition, whatever his faults, lack of determination and sheer guts were not among them. Despite these positive thoughts, no sign of him was found that day and by evening a radio message was sent to that effect and given that we had to consider him missing, the radio-operator assumed the role of Base-Commander.

Another miserable night followed during which the wind and the temperature dropped further. The following morning, with visibility over 300 metres and the drift snow no more than 1 metre high, it was decided to make wide sweeps around the base in the Muskeg tractor as well as sweeping the horizon constantly with binoculars.

It was decided to concentrate particularly on the lines of empty oil drums, which, at Bryan's initiative had been laid to form a line from the base to the coast at the nearest point some 5 kilometres away and a line inland from the base half a kilometre long, intended to serve as an airstrip.

It was from the direction of the airstrip, at about 3 in the afternoon, that the Muskeg tractor, making a wide sweep, reported seeing a grey figure moving slowly and uncertainly toward the base.

It was Bryan, haggard, half-frozen, but unbowed. Once picked up he was brought immediately inside and into the sick bay.

He made a full recovery and, the following day, told us all what had happened, in his own inimitable way. Having switched off and "parked" the radar, he exited from his side and saw "a shadow" moving away from the radar and away from the safety lines.

Thinking that it was me, he ran in that direction, only to find after perhaps only 20 metres, that there was no more shadow, nor was there anything else to be seen, including the radar and the safety lines.

According to his version, he decided to try and find one of the first oil drums in the line which led from the base to the coast, in order to have some idea of where he was.

As he walked, he told us, he deliberately took a longer step with his left leg in order to counter the natural tendency when walking normally to take slightly larger steps with the right than with the left leg, the consequence of which, over time was to turn imperceptibly anti-clockwise and describe a large circle.

After walking for some considerable distance, he found the line of oil drums and walked from one to another until the visibility had become so bad that he could not see the next one.

By this time, the light was fading and he made the decision to dig in to save his life. Using the large bear-paw gloves as scoops, he dug out a hole in the lee of an oil drum and curled up inside it, allowing the snow to cover him and he hoped, keep him warm enough to survive the increasing cold.

He had no idea how long he was there. Even though he was wearing a watch, he did not want to take off the bear-paws, which would have enabled him to see the time. In any case, the

time was somewhat irrelevant. Much more important was trying to stay awake and waiting for the light and the weather to
improve.

Once they did improve sufficiently for him to see the base
lights at night and when daylight came he could see the base
structure, and more importantly he could be seen by others. He
started to walk, or initially stagger, after his long confinement.

His achievement in surviving was remarkable, but typically
he could not prevent himself from embroidering the tale and his
own "Boys' Own" heroism in it.

It appeared that he had walked right past the base, thinking
he was heading for the drum line toward the coast, whereas in
reality he had walked further south and eventually come across
the drum line which marked out the aircraft landing strip.

Some of us later suspected that he had kept awake during
his ordeal by dreaming up ever more pointless projects for the
rest of us to do in the remaining year. It was certainly the case
that the ordeal had neither made him more humble, nor less
of a martinet. The Midwinter play that year was a farce (very
loosely) based on Shakespeare's Julius Caesar—which concerns
a plot to assassinate a tyrant. There are no prizes for guessing
who was cast as Caesar.

Nonetheless, I never saw him in the same black and white
way again. Here was a man, experienced in fieldcraft and lectur-
ing others about the need for safety and common sense in hard
physical conditions, who, in a moment of madness, appeared to
have neglected every precept of common sense in dashing after
a shadow in order to save the life of someone for whom, it had
appeared to me, he had not the slightest liking or regard.

CHAPTER FIVE

The Russians are coming!

Up in the storage loft above the main living quarters was a box full of the flags of all nations. As well as replacement Union Jacks for Halley itself (the base flags did not have a very long life in the blizzard conditions of spring and autumn), there were other flags that we could hoist as a courtesy to visitors from other countries onto the jack staff attached to one of the entrance shafts

Not that we had many such visits, but the previous year a helicopter had flown in from an Argentinian ship taking men and supplies to their base further south named "General Belgrano"—a name that some years later was to become famous, if not notorious—in another context. We had an Argy flag among the stock and so were able to hoist it—at a lower level on the staff than the Union Jack of course.

Halley was in that "slice" of the Antarctic cake which was claimed by 3 countries, namely Britain, Argentina and Chile. Under the Antarctic Treaty, all territorial claims were (an apt term this) "frozen".

The problem which arose this time was that despite much scrabbling around in and around the box, it became obvious that one of the few flags we didn't seem to have was that of the Soviet Union.

This posed a problem for the very good reason that we had heard that we were to receive a visit from the 23rd Soviet Antarctic Expedition ship, which was "passing by" on its way to re victual a Soviet base—Druzhnaya (or "Friendship").

In charge of this expedition was a man who knew our Base Commander, having spent some time with him at the British base of Stonington—known apparently to the Russians thereafter as "Stoningrad".

One of the many things which had impressed the Soviets at Stonington was the fact that one of the huts, for lack of anything better, was literally built on foundations of butter! Well, wooden cases containing a dozen kilo tins of butter at least. This fact apparently impressed the Russian visitor no end.

A radio "sched" with their ship had established contact and a visit had been arranged. But where to get the important flag?

There was only one thing to do—get out the sewing machine and make one.

Fortunately the Soviet flag was not a terribly complicated one—just a red banner with a yellow hammer and sickle in the top left-hand corner. We had plenty of red cloth and some scraps of golden yellow were found. A workaday representation of a sickle was cut out, sewed on to the red cloth and an equally makeshift hammer was then sewn over it with the head of the hammer enclosed by the crescent of the sickle. The flag was then hemmed all round, since the red cloth would have quickly started to unravel at the edges once exposed to the constant wind.

Since we were not at all sure at what time the visitors would arrive, it would have to fly for a few days perhaps before their arrival and during their visit.

The flag, it had to be admitted, looked distinctly amateur and we had some worries that the visitors might find it a little insulting, not only because the workmanship was not exactly haute-couture, but because we had had to make our own, not having the real thing. This was, after all, 1975 and although "detente" had begun between the "west" and the Soviet bloc, the USSR was still a monolithic nuclear power under the "dictatorship of the proletariat"—at this time represented by a septuagenarian former general of very limited faculties called Leonid Brezhnev.

The Cold War was still extant and curiously enough, one of the few places where Cold War relations were warmer than elsewhere was Antarctica. Here was a community of scientists from many nations and in the spirit of scientific cooperation, relations thawed, even if the surroundings didn't. We were not really sure what to expect. What would they be like, these "Soviet men". How would they react to us?

We knew that their ship had come into a portion of the low shelf about 50 kilometres from Halley and that they intended to fly from there. In order to help their landing we were asked to lay out a helicopter landing area and we did so using the obvious and time-honoured method—cocoa.

Probably since IGY in 1957-58 we had cases of truly vile American cocoa powder which no-one liked. It was bitter and like American chocolate, far removed from what we considered to be real chocolate—i.e. Cadbury's.

As a result, it was used to mark our football pitches and in this case, a circular area with a large letter H in the middle. Being dark brown, the powder was as effective on snow as groundsman's white paint on a cricket pitch with the additional effect that it absorbed the sun's heat rapidly and effectively warmed itself into the snow surface so that the initial line became in fact a trough up to 10 centimetres deep.

As we heard that the visitors were approaching we set off a red flare which sent a plume of scarlet smoke in the direction of the wind.

The wind increased mightily, as did the noise as an enormous (to us) Ilyushin MI-8 helicopter hovered overhead and settled right down in the middle of the cocoa landing pad. It was a damn big beast—the type later became known worldwide as gunships in Afghanistan when the USSR got itself disastrously tied up in that geopolitical graveyard.

Out stepped a rugged-looking man who could have been a young American university professor in the late 1950's—handsome, with a winning smile and a crew-cut. This was Garrick Grikurov, head of the 23rd Soviet Antarctic Expedition.

A group of Soviets followed and after perfunctory salutes and shaking hands, were escorted into the base. As they approached the entry shaft, they enthusiastically noticed the Soviet flag and with great enthusiasm on their part and puzzlement on ours congratulated us on such a splendid artefact—we assumed out of excessive politeness.

They entered the base and as they passed through the corridors and huts on the way, politeness gave way to curiosity and they poked their heads into every nook and cranny seeming to find the whole set-up mightily impressive.

Drinks were served and further arrangements made for more visitors to come from their ship and for some of us to visit the ship in return. The chopper had already gone back to bring some more visitors and we had watched as it started its engines—a slow and somewhat cumbersome process it seemed.

The very large rotor-blades were spun by means of a small "donkey-engine" and after some minutes of this, there was a huge roar as the main turbines finally started and took over the work of pushing the rotors round to their maximum speed at which point the beast lifted, pointed forward and screamed up and away.

On base it seemed that Russians swarmed everywhere, some with distinctly Asiatic appearance, others European and some new arrivals were not Russian at all.

With the 23rd Soviet Antarctic Expedition was a group of scientists from the East German "Aerologisches Institut" of Berlin (East Berlin, that is, for the city was still divided).

These perhaps were the most interesting of the visitors since most of the Russians were simple crewmen but these were highly qualified and intelligent scientists who had a great deal more knowledge of the west, though not from much personal experience, than did the Russian crew.

Three of us on base spoke some German. Ken, the radio operator, had very good colloquial "Plattdeutsch", picked up in Hamburg and Bremerhaven when a ship's radio operator. I had school German and had learned grammar and studied some German literature at university, but had nothing approaching Ken's fluency.

The other Ken, our BC, also spoke the language and we were able to learn a lot of the scientists' rather strange existence during their voyage.

Although a part of the expedition, they had, it turned out, led almost completely separate lives from the Russians. They had been aboard ship for a total of 14 months since their departure from Leningrad (now St. Petersburg) and had, amazingly, traversed the Arctic Ocean from there and after a halt in Vladivostok on the Pacific coast, had sailed to Australia and from Fremantle to the Antarctic. During the whole of this time they lived in a container strapped to the deck of the ship and had practically no contact with the crew. There they played their own music, read their own books and visited the rest of the ship only to use the canteen and the toilet facilities.

They had harsh words for both of these. Living for 14 months on a diet which consisted mainly of Shchi (cabbage soup) was no-one's idea of luxury.

They found the toilets so disgusting they tended to go 'over the side' whenever the weather allowed it. At Christmas, they told us, they managed to make a "tree" from bits of sticks and cotton wool and to decorate it with bits of ribbon. The rest of the ship, being Communist, did not celebrate Christmas at all. It all sounded rather sad.

One young man showed photos of himself with shoulder-length hair. He had had to submit to a crew-cut by the Russian barber in Leningrad, since his haircut was regarded as degenerate. The Germans all complained that their colour film had been ruined by being passed through a primitive Soviet x-ray machine.

We gave them Kodachrome, but they had serious difficulty with understanding how they could get it developed. "Just post it to Kodak." we said, unthinkingly, for such things were simply not possible out of what was then Communist East Germany

Finally we reckoned they could have it developed in Australia, which they were visiting again after their stint at Druzhnaya.

Ken the BC had baked "Weihnachtskueche" from his mother's recipe and this spiced Christmas cake took pride of place in a grand buffet which we organised for the guests. For the Germans it was the greatest treat imaginable — Rhine and Moselle wines, sausage rolls, pastries, cold meats and relishes, Löwen-bräu Bavarian beer and a vast range of cakes and biscuits.

In addition we had reading material in German, "Stern" and "Der Spiegel" magazines and suchlike. One of the German scientists ruefully pointed out that all of these were freely available just 20 miles from where he lived, but were as inaccessible as the moon, except that by sailing round the world to Antarctica he could have them for free!

The Russians seemed, apart from Grikurov himself, some-what unsure and uneasy and it was then realised that most of them had no idea what you did at a buffet meal -they had only ever had meals sitting down so the idea of taking a glass of something and circulating while picking out morsels from the buffet was quite alien to them.

During the meal, various plates and cutlery needed washing and one of the German scientists volunteered to help me. We spoke in German as we washed and dried and one of his comments spoke volumes about the relationship between them and the Russians.

"Our friends the Russians" he said,

"Yes?"

"You know, they're not quite European".

CHAPTER SIX

The Russians are here!

Grikurov wanted to invite some of us back to his ship, but needed more fuel for the helicopter. He was astonished to discover that the base generator sets used Avtur (aviation turbine fuel) rather than diesel. The same was true of the base tractors. The diesel engines were specially modified to inject lubrication oil directly into the cylinders, since Avtur is far more refined and less oily than diesel. Diesel has the disadvantage of freezing at minus 15 or so.

A long discussion took place in the lounge around international fuel equivalence tables the result of which was that we ended up fuelling the helicopter with our Avtur.

Since we only had hand pumps, this took some time, but the results were spectacular. Once fuelled up, the guests decided to take us in small groups for trips around the bay. This was a most popular suggestion, since in the two years almost that half of us had been there; we had never seen Halley and its surroundings from the air. The first group got in and the pilot started the donkey-engine which drove the blades around until the main motors started. Whereas this had previously taken some time, this time after a few revolutions there was a bang followed by a tremendous roar and vast quantities of soot shot out of the turbines. The fact was that our generator fuel was far cleaner than their helicopter fuel. We later discovered that they used the same fuel for the helicopter as for the ship's diesels!

More trips around the bay followed and more refuelling with base Avtur. It seemed to be giving the helicopter the equivalent of a re-bore and de-coke.

This was not the only indication we had of what seemed to be a degree of technical simplicity, or lack of sophistication on the part of the Soviets. There were many humdrum items on base by which they were most impressed, to the point of photographing and recording details of, to us, very basic things including storage units in the garage for neatly storing bolts, nuts and spares and the flexible joints made of titanium which took up the vibration between the generator sets, which wobbled when running and the exhaust pipes, which were fixed.

They were all astonished at how young we all were. We were surprised by how old many of them were, but the oddest and saddest thing was the presence of a man of Asiatic appearance who appeared to be without friends and was treated as though he was either a tax-collector or a leper. He was, we discovered, the "Politnik". His job was to keep an eye, on behalf of the Soviet Communist Party, on the rest! The ship had effectively two First Officers, one was the real one and the "Politnik" was the other.

In the base lounge fraternization was going well, the Russians in one group and the East Germans in their own group talking and drinking with us.

The radio operator decided to put on some music and a quick search among the LPs discovered a record of Bavarian beer-drinking songs, like those sung at the Munich Oktoberfest. Soon a group of us were singing along and swinging beer tankards. The Russians were horrified and the atmosphere started to become distinctly chilly. The BC saved the day by diving back into the LP collection and triumphantly emerging with a record of the Red Army Choir, which he rapidly substituted.

Trade loomed large in our relations. The Russians were, it seemed, no more enamoured of the crew diet of cabbage soup than the East Germans were and they were both excited to discover that we had stocks of delights such as tomato ketchup and Tabasco sauce -indeed many things which would spice up their bland diet as well as much-prized Cadbury's chocolate. They also knew and were apparently very fond of — Weetabix — of all things.

41

They were also extremely keen to get hold of western cigarettes and whisky. Given that their "Lenin" cigarettes appeared to be made of sweepings from the tobacco shed floor this was not surprising. What was surprising was the capacity for trade — we had a stock of getting on for half a million cigarettes on base and no-one smoked! This surplus was caused by years and years of neglecting the annual audit of supplies with the result that the same quantities kept coming year after year, despite a burgeoning surplus. We also had a huge quantity of tinned spinach and managed to convince the Russians that it was a much-prized western delicacy!

In return, we got kilogram tins of beluga caviar, whole Kamchatka salmon in brine and Crimean champagne (all from the Russian officers' stores, not for the crew!) On the negative side we also got barrels of sauerkraut.

Finally a group of us flew out to their ship. The ship was moored off the Low Shelf some 15 miles away and looked quite presentably modern. It was, we discovered, built in Finland in the late 1960's as part of war reparations (WW2) to Russia.

While in the helicopter, I had cut the back of my hand on a protruding piece of poorly finished metal and the cut was bleeding profusely under the handkerchief I had wound around it.

Once aboard, I was hustled by a rather sinister little bald man along a corridor and down some stairs. Stopping at a double door, he took out a key and opened it, ushered me inside and then turned and locked the door behind us both. Around us were medical devices and bottles which made it apparent that this was the ship's sick-bay. He motioned me to sit in a dentist's chair and then opened some cupboards. "Omigosh", I thought. "They have found out that I worked for the Ministry of Defence before joining BAS. He'll inject me with a truth drug!"

Nothing so painless. He came back with a bottle of dark brown fluid and proceeded to pour concentrated Iodine on the cut! I was in agony. After a contented "Humph" he returned with a Soviet sticking plaster which, after drying the wound, he pressed over the cut with a flourish. To my intense relief he then opened the door and led me out, locking it carefully behind him.

I later discovered that the reason for the high security in the sick bay was to prevent crew members from stealing the medicinal alcohol — unlike the officers, they were not allowed vodka!

After ten minutes the Soviet sticking plaster quietly fell off.

The ship's corridors and rooms were decorated with red banners with Cyrillic exhortations printed on them "Workers of the world unite!" and similar messages. When we asked the crew what they meant they seemed somewhat embarrassed and paid them little attention, nor did they seem to think that we should. They were fixtures and fittings just like bulkheads and fire-extinguishers.

Turning a corner a sight took our very breath away. Three delightful young ladies stood in front of us. These were the first real ladies (young or old) that some of us had seen in 18 months. Perhaps they were not in reality as delightful and comely as it seems now, but after 18 months in close proximity to rather hairy men, it was a revelation. We were briefly introduced. Their names, Natasha, Maria, possibly Anastasia, were like something from Tolstoy and they were there to cook for and serve the officers.

We were invited by the poor unpopular "Politnik" to visit his cabin, which a few of us did with some trepidation. He showed us photographs of his wife and daughter, offered us each a shot of vodka. Overall it was a very pleasant little visit except for the rather off-putting loaded Kalashnikov on his bed, with the safety catch off. Nothing could have made his unpopularity aboard ship clearer, for the Kalashnikov was not intended to deter foreigners, but his own shipmates.

We met the Captain in a lounge below the bridge. On the wall were three portraits — Marx, Engels and Lenin. Our cook, whose strong point, fortunately, was cooking rather than history or politics walked up to Lenin's portrait and said approvingly

"Ah......, Stalin!"

Somewhere behind us, a pin dropped. We all trooped out as fast as possible.

We found ourselves in the officers' mess where a superb banquet of marinated salmon, rye bread, cabbage, caviar, champagne and vodka awaited us. A multiplicity of toasts followed

"To world peace!"

"Na Zdaroviye!"

"To friendship between nations!"

"Na Zdoraviye!"

"To wives and girlfriends—may they never meet!"

"Na Dzoraviye!"

"To vodka!"

"Za drovya!"

"Da Razvuye!"

Every time a toast was proposed, we all had to stand and drink a glass of Stolichnaya vodka in one gulp.

Soon, standing became increasingly difficult, people started laughing, people started singing, and some started crying.

It's hard to remember what happened after that, but we did get back in the helicopter. The pilot, who was also singing, managed to get us back to base and what seemed a few days later, some of us emerged.

When they left, the Russians took the Soviet flag we had made, because, as they explained, it was so much better than their own! This was true; their own flag was made of very inferior cloth with the hammer and sickle painted on.

It wasn't all they took.

We later discovered that practically every copy of Penthouse, Playboy and other such magazines containing tasteful pictures of naked ladies had mysteriously vanished—as had our copies of "A day in the life of Ivan Denisovich" and "The Gulag Archipelago"—our only copies of Alexander Solzhenitsyn's novels.

For days afterwards the cook simply put out Russian champagne and caviar at breakfast. Of course the time came when one of our number, coming in for breakfast spoke the immortal line:

"Shit. Not bloody caviar and champagne for breakfast again!"

CHAPTER SEVEN

The bog chisel.

It was a simple tool, a kind of mason's chisel head of mild steel with a socket so that it fitted onto the end of a wooden broom handle. An invaluable part of kit when travelling, it was used to probe the snow.

Crevasses were found at particular places, usually where there was differential movement of the ice sheet. Near the coast were the "chips"- indentations, where the ice sloped down to the sea. At each side of the "chip", stretching back inland, were zones of weakness and crevassing.

In good light, with a low sun and high contrast it was possible to make out the outlines, where snow, forming the bridge of the crevasse, was slightly depressed compared to the surrounding surface.

Inland, the most notorious area was the so-called "Hinge Zone", where the ice shelf came off underlying rock and floated on the sea 500 feet below. The movement of the shelf supported on water, compared to the immobility of land-supported shelf caused a zone of intense fracturing, where very large crevasses existed.Early on after the arrival of the new intake, the new Base Commander, who had a wealth of experience as a General Assistant (GA) on the Antarctic Peninsular and had done much sledging with dogs, insisted that we all visit a local crevasse and descend into it using ropes, jumars and electron ladders to see for ourselves the danger, and beauty of it.

Beautiful it was. After making a simple hole and enlarging it with the crevasse probe to about the diameter of a man, an electron ladder was fixed into solid ice a few metres away and uncoiled into the hole. Fixed ropes were installed and, using hand-held jumars, the BC descended into the hole. After reconnoitring the hole, he called up for others to follow. Inside was pastel pale blue in a hundred subtle shades and we stood on a solid bridge inside the crevasse marvelling at the sight. Further on the bridge was no more and we could gaze into a huge space the size, it seemed, of a cathedral nave.

Falling into one of these, the chances of survival were slim, even if you survived the initial fall. That was why the crevasse probe was such an important tool. It was essential to gauge the strength and dimensions of what you were about to either cross, or go around—depending on what you found.

Occasionally you would fall victim to a "man-trap" where the pressure of the feet would open up a hole just the diameter of the victim who, to his great surprise, would find his view suddenly transformed from that of 6 feet above the ground, to that of 6 inches when most of his body disappeared into the hole leaving him trapped and supported by his arms on the flat surface of the Bundu.

In this circumstance, it was advantageous to be carrying a crevasse probe so that, if you were quick enough, you could turn it horizontal and use it as a support across the snow surface. Once trapped, it usually required the help of others to get out. Try thrashing about and the diameter of the hole would simply increase, enabling the shoulders to fall through as well. In cases where you had fallen into a crack whose width diminished with depth, you would simply move further down and getting out was made harder. In cases where the hole was in a crevasse bridge, there could well be a monstrous cavern underneath you in which your legs were suspended, effectively on the roof. Move too much and you would fall through to oblivion.

Fids on other BAS bases and English-speaking polar explorers and mountaineers all called a crevasse-probe a crevasse-probe. At Halley Bay was it called a "Bog Chisel."

The reason for this was twofold. Firstly, the peculiar sanitary arrangements at Halley and secondly the fact that the implement was used much more often in relation to these, rather than in relation to exploring and travelling, which had ceased at Halley except as personal free-time activities.

The base was a series of huts encased in tunnels made of Armco, galvanised corrugated steel. These had been built on the ground, or at least in shallow channels and had later become buried.

In 1972-3, the construction year, a team of Royal Marines from the Falklands had come to the site and dug a most important hole, some 25 feet square and 40 feet deep next to the line which would become the tunnel joining the kitchen hut to the dormitory hut.

It was to become the base loo, the john, the netty, the smallest room, the place of easement, or more usually "The Bog".

Built over the hole was a small hut, not encased in Armco, but linked by an Armco tunnel to the tunnel connecting the kitchen and dorm blocks. The hut was divided into two small rooms. In each a top-and-tailed 45-gallon drum was inserted into the floor and on top of the drum was placed a comfortable wooden toilet seat. Excretions fell into the depths of the cold pit.

The hut was not heated. Had it been, there was a distinct risk that the surrounding ice would melt, in particular the ice which supported the hut from underneath, with the disastrous consequence that the hut itself, with whoever might be occupying it, would fall into the depths of the pit. "Going", especially in the night, was not a comfortable experience and in pyjamas, not one you would want to linger over. There was no reading material in the cubicles, it was a strictly business affair.

A wag from the previous year had designed motifs on the doors of the two cubicles. One a vertical sword surrounded with flames, the other a blushingly modest white rose, with drops of blood on the petals.

The symbolism was obvious, but the designation pointless, since the base was all male. A consequence of the design was a distinct preference of base personnel to use the left-hand cubicle—the one with flaming sword, over the right-hand one with the white rose. This preference had long-term effects.

As stated, excretions fell into the frozen depths, but gravity being what it is; they tended to fall in one area, directly below the toilet seat. Over time, the result was the creation of a frozen stalagmite (some used another spelling).

The frozen creation increased over time in girth, but more ominously, in height, so that ultimately it entered the lower part of the oil-drum cylinder, where the top could be clearly seen from the rim of the toilet seat.

It reached the stage where there was a real fear that the thing would grow up to within very close proximity of one's rear end when sat upon the throne — not a pleasant prospect.

And thus the bog-chisel was born. A crevasse probe was left in each cubicle to enable users to hack off the top of the stalagmite and with luck, send it tumbling to the far depths.

For nearly two years this worked. Solid hacking with the bog-chisel would usually send 3-4 feet of stalagmite tumbling down below.

Nonetheless, more always seemed to build up than regular hacking would remove and the top of the thing grew inexorably upward until it entered the metal tube which descended directly from the seat and which was in fact the 45-gallon oil drum with the ends cut out.

This made for difficulties. The restricted space made it much harder to attack the object with the bog-chisel and even if you succeeded in cutting off the top, there was no room left for it to fall into the depths. Something had to be done.

The task fell to the new intake of Fids, those who had only been at Halley a year. The "old guard" had hardly 6 months to go before shipping out and home and none was willing to contemplate any kind of action to solve a problem which would no longer affect them.

Not many of the rest were either. The only solution was for someone to be lowered into the pit with the necessary tools to cut the stalagmite down at the very base. A sort of lumberjack job, but whereas the lumberjack is in the fresh air surrounded by the beauty of the forest and the smell of fresh pine needles, the kind of lumberjack required here would work in very different conditions.

The "trees", of which there were only two, were vertical concretions of the unmentionable with, as a substitute for leaves, white toilet paper. The floor of the pit was full of hidden horrors and there was practically no light.

The heroic volunteer would have to be lowered down into this on a rope with the appropriate tools and a torch. His condition, when and if he emerged, would be quite disgusting and immediate measures would have to be taken.

Needless to say, Fids did not rush forward to volunteer. It is fair to say that those who were normally never reticent about anything else and indeed could be regarded as possessing a fair degree of "braggadocio", not to say a big mouth, were exceptionally quiet when it came to this matter.

Salvation, as is often the case, came from an unexpected quarter. A Geophysicist, a quiet, unassuming, gentle youth with a penchant for making complex model ships and who normally wouldn't say boo to a goose announced suddenly that he would do it.

He did it. This humble hero was lowered, wearing old sledging clothes, into the pit and in record time sawed through the monstrous towers, sending both crashing down to the floor and surviving the process.

He was extricated and hurried away to dispose of the clothing.

After an exceedingly long shower and a change into new clothes, he modestly sat at the bar and was feted to the rafters by the entire base.

"It was nothing," he said. "A piece of cake."

CHAPTER EIGHT

The icing on the cake.

Midwinter.
The sun left us at the end of May, only to return at the end of August. Three months of darkness and intense cold followed. Although the base was underground and had no windows and therefore only artificial light, it did make a difference—quite a large one for some.

Any exit from the base was dark and cold. The maximum light from the sun was a very faint, though beautiful, red glow on the horizon at midday, when there was no cloud. The lack of sunlight definitely had an effect on the psyche and some individuals were more affected than others. For some, depression was a problem and homesickness may have kicked in for perhaps the first time. Normal base life continued of course, but fuel runs were done in the dark and bitter cold, fingers got jammed between oil drums, things tripped one over, tempers frayed and small problems tended to assume larger proportions.

Of course there was some relief. The place was never totally dark. The Aurora could put on the most spectacular displays and often did. On occasion you could hear it. It is difficult to believe, but the Aurora can make a whistling, rustling, "shooshing" sort of noise.

On a late night trip to the balloon shed a quiet arc—the first manifestation of an auroral display—had been doubling and moving back and forth, occasionally sending out streamers and then changing colour from green through blue and violet while at the same time moving up in the sky and becoming ever more frenzied in its activity as it started to assume the corona shape which tended to signify the height of the display as red and

50

violet streamers danced around, forming a series of coronets. In this case, the climax of the display appeared around the zenith and it began to fade, as it usually did, back to a quiet arc on the horizon of greenish colour and finally disappearing. This time it did something spectacularly different.

Instead of retreating quietly, a sudden transformation created lapping waves of green light covering the entire sky—the impression was that which a fish might get by observing silver waves across the surface of the water from a point far below. It was magnificent almost beyond description and was accompanied, like sea waves, by a noise—a sort of papyrus rustling sound as the green "waves" lapped the velvet sky.

During the winter, time tended to lose some of its meaning. For those such as the meteorologists and geophysicists, there were schedules, which had to be strictly adhered to—observations at set times, maintenance and calibration at regular intervals and in some cases particular times of day.

Likewise the radio operator had strict schedules to maintain.

For others—the diesel mechanic, the tractor mechanic, the base doctor perhaps, the necessary work could be done whenever they felt like doing it and in some cases it was advantageous to work at night, when the base electrical load was lower, for example and the tractors not required. Thus it was that the daily routine was more or less inverted for some members of the team and the lonely vigil of the night meteorologist was enlivened by the waking presence of a few others, doing their own thing.

The winter was not by any means all gloom. The extreme clarity of the Antarctic air, plus the high albedo or reflectivity of the snow surface means that any light is amplified and so it was possible, on a clear day or night to read a newspaper by starlight alone. The planet Venus, which is quite visibly prominent in mid-latitudes, was so bright in Antarctica as to cast a shadow.

If there was a moon, the light was even more impressive and a full moon at night was truly a wonderful experience—giving the impression that, if temperatures had been higher, moonbathing would have been a pleasant activity. Certainly those whose daily routine had shifted or inverted were occasionally to be seen taking the dogs for a midnight run in the brilliant light of the moon.

When the sky was clear, but the air was supersaturated, we got "precipitation in a clear sky", otherwise known to generations of Fids as "diamond dust". The entire air was filled with tiny, highly reflective ice crystals, which led to a whole series of amazing optical phenomena. In bright sunshine there would be "sun-dogs" or parhelia, two points of light each 23 degrees either side of the sun and often split into rainbow hues. In very good conditions, you got an arc around the sun and possibly a second arc. In exceptional cases, there was a false sun 180 degrees away from, that is opposite, the real one. When these phenomena occurred at night with a full moon, they were ineffably beautiful and because the light was more subtle, superior than those of the sun. They were called parselenae as opposed to parheliae.

Time outside was limited. Base work such as the lifting of oil-drums and transport to the generator shed was cruelly cold at times and the manhandling of 45 gallon drums at minus 40 or 45 degrees was a considerable trial. Any contact with bare metal, even when wearing inner gloves and sledging gloves was painful. Breathing hard was painful and exhaled breath encrusted any beard with ice and misted over any goggles so that seeing was difficult. You always knew how cold the air was, without a thermometer; simply by looking at the generator shed exhaust. The gases, though coming out at high temperature and normally rising high into the air, would become a horizontal plume immediately on reaching the end of the exhaust pipe.

The dogs, usually kept outside on the spans were brought inside if the temperature remained at 40 or below for a week or more. They would be tied at the base of the shafts, where the temperature was about minus 5—in these conditions, they became too hot and panted frequently. Outside, everyone moved more slowly. In very low temperatures, even rapid walking could cause an effective wind and the wind-chill would increase, with a consequent risk of frost-nip.

The buddy system was used while working outside. One would observe the other to look for tell-tale patches of white skin on exposed parts of the face. If observed, these had to be warmed quickly before the skin became dead, if warmed later the recirculation of the blood into the affected area would cause considerable pain.

Measurements to detect the movement of the ice shelf using star positions were a trial in these conditions. The eyebrows tended, if you were not careful, to stick solidly to the theodolite eyepiece and prising them off by your companion's breathing on them freed the eyebrows alright (always minus some hairs), but iced up the eyepiece. Turning the theodolite and reading the circles was a difficult exercise wearing thick gloves and required immense patience, which was not always to hand.

It was far from unknown for a frozen Fid, after half an hour of immobile exposure outside to head straight for the kitchen on entering the base and lie fully stretched out on top of the Aga cooker until thawed sufficiently to bend.

Many of the spare time activities were confined to indoors where various vehicles would be maintained and in some cases restored to life. Nansen sledges would be repaired in readiness for the return of the sun and the possibility of travelling. Hobbies of various kinds provided solace—making models, learning skills, writing diaries, and developing film. It was traditional at Midwinter for each base member to make a present to be given to another base member (by random selection) and this was taken very seriously by most and done in the greatest secrecy and in some cases with enormous dedication and hard work producing items of great quality and originality.

As well as the making of presents, most people had hobbies, whether making model boats (but where to sail them?), or renovating one of the stock of curious old vehicles left over the years. Neither the diesel nor tractor mech had anything to do with this activity—too much like a busman's holiday.

We were able to develop our own colour slides using the Kodak Ektachrome process. It was messy, involved precise timing and really needed very clear water, which we didn't have.

Of course our water, being melted snow, was very clean and certainly harboured no life forms inimical to good health. However it did, as a natural consequence of being melted in a tank, contain elements of dust and grit. These, though very small, were quite enough to constitute a "bleg"—a Fid word meaning an imperfection on a slide.

Much effort was put into filtering water through blotting paper to try to eliminate this plague, but it was never possible. Many were the proud Fids who during a slide competition would be subject to the cry "Bleg!" when one of these was spotted.

The competitive slide shows held in the lounge are worth a mention in themselves. Never was a more critical and voluble audience assembled. Not only did practically everyone take hundreds, if not thousands of photos (excepting Ee, the diesel mech, who seemed immune), but there was a limited choice of subject matter, which everyone had to use.

The result was perhaps the most critical slide show known to man. Everyone tried to get a new angle on the limited range of subjects leading to "artistic" shots of, for example, the balloon shed looking down, the balloon-shed looking up, the balloon-shed from the side, the same in evening light, the same with hoar frost and so on, ad nauseam. Efforts to "artify" scenes became horrible clichés—a favourite being crossed ski sticks hiding the sun. Attempts at "heroic explorer" poses were guaranteed to produce hilarious scorn, while a really beautiful scene would be immediately denigrated as "chocolate boxy", to indicate the type of photo so beloved of chocolate assortment makers.

You couldn't win whatever you tried and so any slide show was a chorus of "Rubbish!" "Bleg!" "Chocolate boxy!", "Cliché!" and worse. The same photos shown to admiring friends and relations at home would have produced a chorus of ooohs and aaahs and admiring applause.

Much time was spent mounting slides in glass mounts—very expensive, but "guaranteed" to preserve and flatten the film to conserve it longer. They were not very successful. First of all they would trap microscopic dust and hair particles between the two halves of the mounting. You could only see these when the slide was projected, and what was worse, when the heat of the projector bulb heated the slide sufficiently the "blegs" came alive, twitching and oscillating like bacilli with flagellae. A "bleg" was bad enough—a moving "bleg" was the object of utter derision.

Much time and effort was consecrated to the production of the traditional "Midwinter Play". It was always a farce, even when it was not intended to be and was put on by the newcomers for the oldsters, which meant that about 8 people were in the cast and 8 or 9 in the audience. The audience, of course, had put on their own performance the year before and were not prepared to be outdone. The cast started off at a disadvantage.

Some Midwinter plays even had scripts, though to get the cast to learn them proved impossible.

In 1974 the play was a (very loose) version of Julius Caesar intended as a satire on Bryan, the base-commander, who had a reputation as a martinet. This meant that costumes were quite easy (a toga is easily created from a bed sheet) and the script posed less of problem since it was printed out on telex paper and rolled into a Roman scroll, which every member of the cast carried.

Complete with versions of songs from Gilbert and Sullivan, the whole thing was to follow (not a good idea) the Midwinter Feast—a 14 course banquet of largely tinned goodies washed down with a great deal of booze.

Booze was a slightly controversial subject. Essentially we had enough high quality booze in stock to float the base away, but this had, a year or so previously, earned the disapproval of the then Director, Sir Vivian Fuchs.

Each base had a very civilized allocation of bar drinks essentially amounting to a bottle of gin, a bottle of whisky, a bottle of vodka, a bottle of rum and perhaps another spirit or two per man per year. That meant 18 of each! In addition there was a crate or two of wine and a crate or three of beer per man per year. Since some people didn't drink (not many) and some years drank less than others, a stock built up on base, which would have done credit to a distillery.

In addition, each Fid was free to buy his own booze on board ship from Eric, the ever-obliging Chief Steward. A bottle of Glenfiddich single malt from the ship's bond cost 67 pence.

The result was that we would flambé pancakes in Glenfiddich.

There was also the notorious Monteplonk — Uruguayan wine from Montevideo sold in gallon jars with basketwork holders.

To say that Monteplonk was rough would be understating the case considerably. The red was drinkable — the white so disgusting that its only real use would be as paint-stripper.

As well as the multiplicity of courses at the banquet, the highlight of the festivities was centred on the Midwinter Cake. Another old Fid tradition, every year the cook attempted to outdo the previous year's effort.

This tendency, though motivated by aspirations to excellence, eventually fell victim to over-ambition and this was a classic case.

The cook had decided on a cake which would be a map of the base with, in the centre, the landscape of drift snow, the radio aerial (or conical monopole as it was technically known) with representations of tractors, oil drums, dunnage lines and other base paraphernalia exquisitely rendered using icing sugar, pipe –cleaners and other arcane aspects of the patissier's art.

The whole was to be encircled by the name of the base "Halley Bay 1974" with each letter and number a cake in its own right.

The cook worked and slaved lovingly producing each letter and number in cake and icing and keeping them all for the final assembly. The central part was put together, the decorations minutely crafted, the conical monopole erected and the dunnage lines laid out with spun sugar, the icing oil drums coloured black, the tractors red with cochineal — it was all splendid.

The dining room was about 16 feet by 16 with a shelf along the kitchen side and a hatchway. In the opposite corner were two long tables along the walls, effectively "L" shaped but for a passage, which bisected the tables in the corner and allowed access to both.

While calculating the final assembly of the cake a momentous discovery was made. The finished cake would be 8 feet in diameter and would cover ¾ of the tables' surface. This was, in itself, not a problem since the cake would appear at the end of the meal after the rest of it had been cleared away.

The problem was where to keep the cake in the meantime! An 8 foot diameter wooden base with the assembled cake upon it would not fit through the door, even vertically, had it been possible to hold it vertically, which it wasn't.

Oh dear! The cook was devastated. In planning the cake he had omitted to calculate the final size of the assemblage.

The finest minds were brought in to consider the issue, Geophysicists and Ionosphericists pondered and calculated. There were some who muttered that these were hardly the finest minds, but it was a Beastie-man (Ionosphericist) who came up with the solution.

It was as unconventional as it was simple. Four holes were cut into the ceiling. Through the holes nylon cords were passed to a colleague in the attic above who tied them to beams. Pulleys were attached and the nylon cords wound around the 4 block mini pulleys. They, in turn were attached to the 8-foot circular base of the cake and with the whole base crowding in to watch, the entire cake was lifted to within a foot of the ceiling, where the nylon cords were tied off. There it remained, suspended.

The meal took place beneath the cake. After the table had been cleared and the champagne brought out, the nylon cord was untied and slowly and magnificently the cake descended onto the table.

Afterwards, it was raised again amid witty remarks that if only the cook had used self-raising flour this would not have been necessary.

It took from July to the end of November to eat it.

Personnel lift

Digging out the Faireyplane

Muff and Brae meet an Emperor

4 Inside a crevasse

With Emps and chick

The Russians (author with E German scientist)

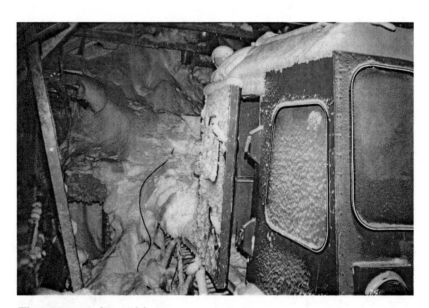

The garage after a blow

Graham Chambers

Formal midwinter Dinner

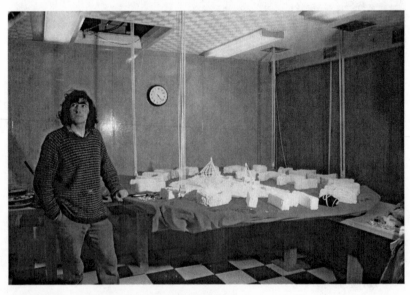

The Cake suspended from the ceiling

Midwinter Play

The Old Ship Bar

Posing as a rugged explorer

Practice streak with astonished builders

Eliason maintenance

Graham Chambers

Fire! Wooden packing cases November 5th

Ship's officers and Ella Woodfield with locals

CHAPTER NINE

Streak!

Perhaps the 1970's was a strange decade, or at least stranger than most. However, much evidence points to the 1950's and 1960's also being strange decades, not to mention those which have come afterwards.

Whatever the case, there was in the 70's a curious tendency for people all over the world who in other respects appeared to be perfectly normal (whatever that may mean) to divest themselves of all clothing in public and run. The running could be across a football pitch, a cricket pitch, a field or a car park—the important thing appeared to be that the place had to be public— the more public the better.

Hence the outbreak of naked runs across sports arenas in full view of the media and in public places in full view of the public. In one famous case, a naked man was apprehended by a police constable while running across a football pitch and his exposed manhood deftly hidden from public view by the constable's smart use of his police helmet to cover the offending article. This probably rather exaggerated the size of the article concerned and perhaps gave the man rather more favourable publicity than that to which he was legitimately entitled.

The practice was also rife of hanging one's naked posterior either out of a vehicle window or simply pointing it at the world at large. This was known as "mooning", whereas the naked run was known as "streaking".

Eventually most fads in the rest of the world percolated down to the Antarctic just as heavy metals and DDT do and we heard over the radio "sched" that the entire South African base at SANAE, all 20-odd of them had performed a mass full-frontal streak before the cameras.

Not long afterwards the news came through that two less-than -intrepid souls had streaked "around the world", by running naked in high summer around the vertical "barber's pole" with a mirror sphere on top, which denotes the precise geographical South Pole at the US base there.

Discussions took place at Halley as to how we could keep our end up (in a manner of speaking). Around the world was out of the question since we were situated about 800 km from the pole. Discussion about a mass streak was not only received with a distinct lack of enthusiasm, but would have been point-less anyway, since we were only 18 in total.

Immortality in the form of an imagined entry in the "Guin-ness Book of Records" loomed and the only possible way this could be achieved was for someone to attempt the coldest streak.

Both the mass streak at SANAE and the "round the world" streak at Pole Station had been achieved at what we rugged Fids considered to be sub-tropical temperatures—the kind of tem-peratures experienced at other BAS bases such as South Georgia or Signy known dismissively by us as "the banana belt".

Such hubris on our part was bound to lead to a fall which took the form of someone being gradually inveigled into carry-ing out the reckless deed as discussion continued.

Naivety combined with excessive enthusiasm on the part of the ultimate victim aided and abetted by carefully calculated stroking of the victim's ego by the rest of the discussants (who might well have plotted it all beforehand) led ultimately to one fool undertaking to do the deed, supported by nothing but the good wishes, combined with a great deal of ribaldry, of the others.

The selected fool was me.

There was no getting out of it. The commitment having been made, the ribbing to which I would have been subjected had the run not taken place would have been unbearable. Rehears-als had to begin. There was to be no messing about. We would wait for the coldest day of the winter and when the temperature

69

hit a record low, the deed would be done with a 200 yard dash from the entrance closest to the garage to the entrance closest to the doctor's surgery—in case perhaps of necessary emergency treatment being required afterwards.

Autumn had begun and the temperatures were getting progressively lower as the sun started to disappear. The first rehearsals involved going out to do the meteorological observations at the Stevenson Screen wearing mukluk canvas boots, running shorts, a short-sleeved tennis shirt and gloves to protect against touching metal surfaces.

Before recording the observations at the Stevenson Screen a run around the radio aerial, known as the "Conical Monopole" served as practice.

The boots did not allow for fast movement and were soon exchanged for running shoes since in temperatures of minus 20 and below, speed was essential, even if it increased the wind-chill factor on a calm day by creating a wind. Getting it over with as quickly as possible was quickly adopted as the campaign strategy. The shoes froze solid and running in them was a curious sensation. On calm days, breath froze and the incipient beard became encrusted with white hoar frost.

The question of beards was an old one in Antarctic history.

Not so much on the later bases, where a shower-room and a supply of hot water made daily shaving less of a chore, but on the earlier bases and when in the field a decision had to be made—whether to waste heat and time melting snow to allow a wet shave (in the early days there was none other) or to let the beard grow.

The disadvantage of the latter was that outside in very cold weather breath froze on the beard, particularly if you were subject to exertion. The resulting icicles on the beard were known as "gombles". Once back in the warmth of the tent or hut, the beard would start to thaw with hours of dripping onto your shirt or down your front—most unpleasant. Attempting to remove the ice on a beard (known to us as de-gombling) was a trying, even painful experience.

When practice running, I decided to shave. Regular runs in shorts and T shirt continued throughout the Antarctic autumn until I could manage a reasonably fast run at minus 20, even with bit of wind, which drastically increased the chill factor.

It was time for a full trial without the shorts and T shirt.

Shoes still had to be worn. It was simply too risky to go barefoot. Excruciating experience with, of all things, a toffee apple had earlier sent a warning shot when the extremely cold fork on which the remains of the toffee apple were impaled, actually froze to my tongue. It had to be carefully unstuck indoors while warming, otherwise part of the very sensitive skin of the tongue would have come off with it. The very thought of it is still awful 30 years later.

A bright and sunny day was chosen after a night shift and, carefully checking that the coast was clear I crept silently up the ladder of a lesser-used shaft and down the other side and commenced a fast run toward the distant shaft at the other end of the base. It was too late to do anything about it when I saw the snow sledge for transporting ice to the water melt-tanks and Dermot the builder innocently shovelling snow into it.

His face, as he saw me in the altogether dashing past him was a picture to behold. Alas he was not the only base member around and the next person I saw climbing out of a shaft had a camera!

The picture was taken and remains the only one of the event since the final coldest attempt was in darkness and conditions inimical to the taking of photographs. It is not an impressive picture. The male member at those temperatures almost disappears and so prurient interest is most definitely lacking.

As Midwinter 1974 approached the base was in almost permanent darkness, more so when cloud covered the sky. We lost the sun and all that was visible was a deep red glow on the horizon around midday. Hatches were battened down, outside activity was limited to fuel runs, snow runs for melt water and gash runs where the accumulated base garbage was taken away to the dump.

All sorts of interior activities were indulged in—model making, sledge maintenance, small vehicle maintenance for hobbies and preparations for the Midwinter festivities involving a play, an enormous feast, a midwinter magazine, the presentation of home-made gifts and many other associated activities.

Finally we hit a period of clear skies and extremely low temperatures. The two dogs were brought into the connecting tunnel, where of course they were too warm, but the temperature outside was below minus 40 for over two weeks and getting colder.

As well as secret preparation for the naked run when no-one was around some of us went skiing behind a muskeg tractor, which could have a fair turn of speed.

At temperatures below minus 40 this was a real trial. Despite being swathed in many layers of clothing, the part of the face around the eyes needed to be uncovered in order to see. The experience was similar to being high-pressure sandblasted and the snow grains, at that temperature, were as hard as diamond. In addition the snow surface was carved by the wind into small ruts and dunes called by the Russian term "sastrugi". these were as hard as concrete and skiing over them was particularly hard on the knees.

Temperatures continued to fall and it soon became clear that we heading for a record low at Halley Bay when the temperature fell one day to minus 48 and the following day passed minus 50. It continued to get colder and we passed the previous record for Halley. The moment for action had arrived.

The radio operator sent the daily meteorological readings to a collection centre where they were recorded together with readings from around the world. When the temperature hit minus 55.3 it was decided to try for the record of the coldest "streak". Various members of base gathered at the tops of the shafts and outside with cameras to record the event. The temperature was officially attested by the Base-Commander and the radio operator and finally I emerged dressed in nothing but running plimsolls and a duvet jacket. Climbing up the ladder to the top of the shaft was accompanied by some distinctly underhand photography of my undercarriage from below. Finally at the top of the shaft I threw down the duvet jacket and ran like hell from one end of the base to the shaft at the other end.

The shock of the cold was amazing, but did not actually feel cold so much as painful, almost like a reverse burning sensation. The blitz of flash bulbs following me was almost blinding, but reaching the end shaft I disappeared down it as fast as a rat up a sewer and ran into the surgery where blankets awaited.

The event was officially recorded and signed by the BC and Radio Operator and I went for in for interior as well as exterior warming.

A telex was sent off to the McWhirter organisation which published the "Guinness Book of Records".

We had to await their verdict for months since it would come to us by mail when the ship arrived in December for the base relief.

In the meantime, the Midwinter festivities lifted all our spirits and finally in late August Spring arrived, the sun returned and base life resumed its more active phase.

It did not seem long before December and midsummer arrived and we bathed in unheard of high temperatures, sometimes approaching zero (from below).

Finally the ship arrived, deliberately crashing into the ice front to drop the mailbags off the bow, the very first things to arrive at base. The arrival of the mail was always a big event.

Distribution was frantic and everyone headed off to read his own mail. After looking at mail from nearest and dearest, I found letter from the "Guinness Book of Records". Tearing it open I went along to the radio shack where I read out the contents.

"Dear Sir," it said:

"Thank you for the information about the streak carried out at a temperature of minus 55.3 degrees centigrade at the British Antarctic Survey Base of Halley Bay.

Although full of admiration for your feat, I regret to inform you that it can not be included in the Guinness Book of records because it has not been recognised as a competitive event.

Yours faithfully,"

Words failed us.

CHAPTER TEN

Lime juice cordial.

Sir Vivian Fuchs, former Director of the British Antarctic Survey and an Antarctic legend, was not amused.

He stood looking at a cargo sledge headed for Halley Bay from the berth of the *Bransfield* at the Low Shelf, some 50 kilometres from the base. Ice conditions were such that this was the only place for unloading to take place and this meant tractor trains of sledges taking 8 hours or so to make the journey.

What had upset him was his observation that the particular cargo sledge was carrying quite enormous quantities of booze. All had been legitimately ordered from the ship's bond and payment made to Eric, the outrageously gay Chief Steward and all was quite above-board. However, each base was supplied every year with at least a bottle of every spirit imaginable and given that not all were used by everyone, stocks built up and every base bar was liberally supplied with alcohol.

The cases of beer, whisky, gin vodka, wine and heaven knows what else were the result of individual orders.

Sir Vivian legally could do nothing about this, since the booze was the property of those who had bought and paid for it.

Nonetheless, he was outraged at the sheer quantity involved and used his considerable moral authority to have the sledge unloaded and reloaded with more essential items—such as food for example.

He had been retired for some years as Director but was still a fine figure of a man—trim, neat and healthy with sparkling blue eyes and a weather-beaten face with small red blood vessels visible on his cheeks. As new recruits we had been invited to his home in Cambridge, where we had all played Frisbee on his spacious lawn. He and the New Zealander Sir Edmund Hillary had together achieved the first crossing of the continent of Antarctica in 1957/8 doing much excellent science on the way and he was therefore an iconic figure.

He had two husky dogs in Cambridge and since huskies need much exercise each day, or else they become both fat and stupid, he had a small cart made with bicycle wheels and used this to go shopping, with the dogs pulling the cart. Sad to relate, it was not long before some curtain-twitching neighbour reported him to the RSPCA and astonishingly, he was forbidden on pain of a fine to continue the practice.

He had come down on what turned out to be his last visit to Antarctica. He still played a hard game of squash and drove a rather fine Jaguar "E-type" in British Racing Green. There had been a bit of scare on his trip down, when he contracted a nasty dose of flu, but he had recovered and once in the aseptic climate of Antarctica, flu was no problem.

The booze was re-loaded onto the sledge during the night when Sir Vivian was safely tucked up in bed aboard ship and was unloaded at Halley the following morning. It added to an already considerable quantity. Wine and beer had to be kept up in the loft, where it would not freeze. Spirits could be left in colder places even outside if buried under the snow.

Among the quantities of alcohol unloaded were 5 gallon glass jars of "Monteplonk"—the name given to wine of rather dubious quality bought in Montevideo, the capital of Uruguay, where the *Bransfield* called in on its way south to re-victual. It could be said that "Monty" was the last stop in civilization for us, although it is true that from there we headed for Port Stanley in the Falkland Islands. There was some doubt among us as to whether Port Stanley was civilization.

"Monty" had cheap bars, cheap women and cheap leather goods including coats and jackets that were made to measure within 24 hours. True, a black leather coat made you look like a Gestapo operative, but they were good quality leather and cheap.

Once the initial port formalities were over, leather salesmen swarmed all over the ship together with bar owners, taxi drivers and an assortment of dubious "traders".

Uruguay at that time was a curious place. It had built up a cradle-to-grave welfare state on the back of an enormous beef industry (Fray Bentos, of corned-beef fame, is a town in Uruguay).

However the beef market had declined over the decades and the money was no longer there to support the system, which meant that everything had a rather run-down feel to it and poverty was rather common.

The oddest thing to us was the traffic. Uruguay had extremely high taxes on imported vehicles and produced none of its own. The result was a fleet of vehicles of remarkable vintage. The town buses were diesel Leylands, made in Britain in 1922. Spares being no longer available, the Uruguayans made their own. Some of the buses had millions of miles on the clock.

Car accessories were not subject to the same fierce import taxes—which led to the most unusual sightings—of Ford Model 'T's, for example, with modern add-ons and "go-faster" stripes.

We had a few days stopover in which to hit the town bars, risk all kinds of horrible intimate diseases, which the ship's medical officer took great pleasure in illustrating with a colour-slide show before we disembarked.

One way of having a night out with a young lady of impeccable reputation was through the "Seamen's Mission". There, you could be introduced to delightful young ladies in a highly respectable and risk-free environment, with the sole disadvantage that if you went out with a girl for the evening, it had to be with a chaperone in tow.

Hanky-panky of any kind was definitely out. I was paired with a delightful young girl whose parents had given her (quite innocently) the forename of Gladys. They obviously had never heard of Monty Python, which in the 1970's had made the name (already going out of fashion) quite unusable since it was applied to an aged crone with curlers and a cigarette hanging out of the side of her mouth and a voice like a Dogger Bank foghorn.

One thing you didn't do was mail a postcard home. Uruguay had just been thrown out of the World Postal Union because of a long strike by the postmen (there was much industrial unrest).

After the strike was over, the enormous stockpile of unsent mail was dealt with by the simple but outrageous expedient of burning it. You could send a card by taking it to an airline office and asking them to take it for a small fee.

The large quantities of atrocious "Monteplonk" when drunk, led to many happy, though perhaps not very accurate, reminiscences. Indeed the red was not quite so atrocious as the white. You needed to be pretty oiled-up already to taste the white, which was reminiscent of turpentine and we thought quite capable of being used as a substitute for it.

The red was actually drinkable, following the dictum that a cheap red is better than a cheap white.

However, once the large bottles began to be emptied, it was noticed that the white bottles were reasonably clear, whereas the red ones had a dark brownish red stain on the inside. At one stage, needing to use an empty bottle for some unremembered purpose, someone tried cleaning the inside, first with soapy water, then with a brush, then with boiling water. Finally acid was used and then hot acid. The stains would not budge. We came to the conclusion that the red wine etched glass permanently. What it did to our stomachs was anyone's guess.

Alcohol was so plentiful we never even thought about the possibility of running out of it, even though there were some highly professional topers amongst our number. Pancakes were flambéd in fine Scottish Single Malts.

Around the bar, with its exquisite marquetry and inlaid brass representation of the Antarctic continent, we would almost all get into the "spirit" of the occasion, usually on Sundays, which was scrub-out day and the cook's day off. The base would be meticulously cleaned and then a cold buffet laid out in the lounge which was consumed while listening to records of BBC radio programmes illicitly passed on to us from the Falkland Islands.

It was during one of these sessions that an anguished cry went up that there was no lime juice to add to vodka, nor indeed to anything else alcoholic which was deemed to be improved by it.

It was clear to us that although there could be no such thing as too much alcohol, there was such a thing as not enough non-alcoholic liquids to add to alcohol.

We had a problem.

Manifests and lists were consulted. Each year it was some-one's job to go through all the stocks of food and drink to see what was needed and what was not so that a telex could be sent to HQ and the next shipment of victuals made up accordingly. No-one really liked this job, which entailed counting the stocks of everything in the food tunnels (a cold job) and up in the lofts (a hot and dusty and cramped job).

The result was that the same manifests tended to be sent in every year whatever the consumption of various victuals. The result of this, over time, was a considerable excess of unpopular or unused victuals. Thus it was that we had a stock of over half a million cigarettes in a year when no-one on base smoked. Many of the brands, such as Capstan full-strength, Wills Woodbines and Senior Service were no longer fashionable amongst smok-ers, being very potent and having no filters and originating from the days when smoking was deemed to be good for you. We had a ridiculous amount of unpopular things, such as tinned spinach which everyone hated.

We should have had soft drinks according to the mani-fests, but no-one had any idea where they were. We had a clue however.

It was remembered that during relief — a very busy and con-fusing period when people work long hours and also nights to get everything stocked away in the space of a week, that many crates had been laid out in lines along the bundu and temporar-ily marked by pieces of dunnage (planks used to separate lots of cargo in the ship's hold). These were hammered into the snow surface and marked with black "magic marker", which did not work well in the cold conditions.

In addition, there was not much space on a 10cm wide plank to write down everything which was laid on the snow surface below. This led to some interesting abbreviations.

A staple foodstuff was chicken breasts in jelly, very handy for making chicken casserole, chicken curry or simple chicken sandwiches. These came in big tins with three rings around the tin signifying a quarter, a half and three-quarters full. Once the chicken was used, these cans with one end removed, became "pee-cans" — very useful when "loitering within tent" on camping expeditions, to avoid having to go outside to pee.

A small pee thus become known as a "single ringer", a standard one a "two ringer" and the drinking of much beer resulted in the rare, but impressive, "three ringer".

Cases of these tins of chicken breasts were marked on the dunnage with the brief and expressive description "hen tits". Other equally expressive abbreviations were common.

The resultant lines of cases, marked with the dunnage became over time, entirely covered with snow, as did everything else left on the ground, including tractors.

Since the base was new, and there was consequently much to be done, including finishing the buildings themselves, the additional food stocks were ignored for most of the first year.

The result, when it was decided that soft drinks were absolutely essential to civilised living, was that we were faced with a large area underneath which was a huge collection of food and drink and above which was a much reduced quantity of signage, the dunnage planks having either fallen over and been buried, or snapped off in a gale and in some cases re-positioned in the wrong place.

Finding lime juice cordial amongst all this was the equivalent of discovering the needle in the haystack. An expedition was launched. At least 6 of us roped off a large area and within that rectangle, roped off smaller rectangles which we could walk across side by side in a line and prod the snow ahead with a "bog chisel" a bit like looking for mines, but in this case the target would not or at least should not, explode.

One by one the rectangles were prodded and probed and various interesting things were dug up, some edible, some not. One thing about storing any kind of food out on the snow was that there was no problem with "use-by dates". The constant low temperature ensured that food thus stored would last for ages.

Indeed, one expedition to the old base buried 40 feet below the surface about half a mile away had turned up some tins of stewing steak dated 1955. The contents were used in a steak and kidney pie which was quite delicious.

Finally we struck gold. A box was unearthed with 12 bottles of Roses Lime Juice Cordial. Six were smashed by the cold and the contents had vanished into the snow, but 6 were intact. Very carefully they were taken inside, unpacked from the crate and very slowly brought to room temperature (i.e. zero degrees) from the minus 25 or so degrees which they were outside. The bottles were treated so gingerly and with such respect and care that one would have thought they contained vintage champagne.

A party was held to celebrate!

CHAPTER ELEVEN

Primus Fear.

The base huts, in their corrugated steel Armco tunnels, were linked together underground by smaller Armco tunnels.

These tunnels were cold, since outside the Armco was solid snow and ice and the connecting tunnels were, of course, unheated, although warmer than outside.

The Armco was egg-shaped in section, for strength, and the wide part of the egg was at the bottom. Upon this was built a floor of plywood. The rest of the tunnel was a bright silver colour, being zinc galvanized steel.

It's hard to say what persuaded the Base Commander that it would be a good idea to paint the inside of the Armco connecting tunnels in a particularly un-fetching shade of pale green.

Had he fond memories of childhood hospitalization in the 1950's? Did we have a huge stock of foul green paint that absolutely had to be used?

Or was it an activity recommended in his American management books for keeping expedition members uselessly occupied?

Who can say?

However, as it was said, so was it written and the Ukase was issued that the connecting tunnels would be painted — green.

A slight problem was that the Armco walls were at a temperature of minus 10 at least and paint tended to freeze instantly on being applied. So did the brush — to the extent that the brush was then solidly and permanently affixed to the tunnel wall.

BC's were trained to get around this sort of minor obstacle and so it was decreed that the tunnels to be painted would be heated, a section at a time.

But how to heat them? Electric radiators were out—powerful heat would be required.

Use of the garage space heater (a kind of small rocket engine) was ruled out by the garage mechanic who was rightly very proprietorial about these things.

There were some rumblings of discontent.

After all, the Armco tunnels were supposed to remain cold so as not to transmit heat from the base to the surrounding snow, which would melt, then re-freeze, causing ice pressure points and rams which could and eventually did, buckle, bend and ultimately destroy the nice egg shape of the tunnels.

A most unfavoured job, carried on at more or less the same time, was to squeeze between the huts and the surrounding Armco with an ice axe and, in amazingly cramped and uncomfortable conditions, hack away at any ice which had formed between the wooden huts and the Armco tunnel precisely to prevent heat transmission to the outside snow and ice.

Back to the painting. It was clear that the tunnels would have to be heated for some time before painting could commence. It was also clear that quite a bit of heat would be needed.

The answer the BC (a former sledging man) came up with was the good old Primus stove, used when sledging and camping.

Filled with paraffin and pre-heated with either Meths or a pre-heating tablet, when the thing was pumped up to the highest possible pressure, it could make the heating element glow bright red and almost pale blue, so hot did it become.

It was immensely useful for pre-heating skidoo spark plugs when they were reluctant to start. Unscrew, bring into tent, heat till bright red and run out and screw back in again quick before pulling on the starter cord. Worked like a dream.

Sometimes the Primus was so efficient that kneeling or half standing in a tent brought your head into the torrid zone, which was so hot (and mixed with the aroma of drying, if not burning socks) that it could make you faint clean away.

Not accustomed to doing things by halves, the BC decreed that a whole line of Primuses be set up on shelves made of planks so that a rack of three levels of stoves was constructed with a total of 12 all burning away during the night.

Naturally, they would need to be refuelled occasionally, not to mention looked at to make sure they were not misbehaving in any way likely to result in a fire.

Fire was always the greatest risk on an Antarctic base. A match, held against a wooden packing case in the very dry air of Halley, was enough to set it alight without tinder of any kind. A relative humidity of 16% ensured that.

A fire in the hut, inside an Armco tunnel which had electric fans at either end to blow cold air past the hut and take away any heat which might melt the surrounding snow and ice would be an inferno.

Dousing a fire with water was practically impossible, unless the fire was a small one in a non-flammable waste-paper bin. For one thing, there wasn't enough liquid water. For another, with so much electrical equipment around and no effective earth due to the fact that the base was essentially floating in the surface of an ice-shelf, the consequences could be disastrous.

Insisting on a triple rack of primuses burning all night in a tunnel to heat the walls so that they could be painted a sickly green smacks of tempting Providence to the limit. Let's just say that it was part of human life's rich tapestry.

The guardian of this lunatic arrangement had to be the night-duty meteorologist, since everyone else was, blissfully or otherwise, asleep.

The night shift was carried out in rotation on a weekly basis between the four meteorologists. Most did not like it much. The reversal of the daily routine resulted in a sort of jet-lag, where you really didn't feel at all up to scratch. Just when you had got used to the change, it was back again to normal, except that for the first few days you were "jet-lagged" all over again. It effectively made you inefficient, tired and grumpy for about 9 days out of 30.

There were the nightly 4 hour meteorological observations to carry out, checks on the outside huts and balloon shed and odd jobs of one kind or another. To stay awake and stave off boredom, all kinds of stratagems were used—black coffee, books, making things, "pottering about" and of course, one of the duties of the night met, fire watch !

It was therefore the height of irony that the man responsible for ensuring that the base did not burn down with all his comrades in it was, that particular week, enjoined with the task of keeping 12 Primus stoves burning on a wooden rack in a tunnel on the base.

It was lucky that when the incident occurred, the night meteorologist happened to be in the Met Office, which was next to the tunnel being heated—the tunnel linking the science hut with the garage and opening into one of the access shafts.

A light sort of "whoomph" was heard. Had the night met been anywhere else within the base, or outside, the noise would not have been heard at all. He went to the hut door and opened it.

Flame was all over the triple wooden rack and dripping onto the wooden floor. The rest of the Primuses were still going full blast but one was not—it had burst. Probably old, the weld on the pressurized paraffin reservoir had burst and the pressurized paraffin sprayed out. Trying not to panic, the met. man rapidly looked for a means of dousing the fire.

Were it to burn any longer the other Primuses could well explode and the resulting spray of burning fuel from 11 stoves would be rather hard to deal with.

Glancing around he saw, on the floor, a bucket of water. Grabbing it, he threw the contents over the burning shelving.

Nothing prepared him for the subsequent shock. Instead of hissing and spitting and steaming, the water burst into flames and covered even more of the shelving and floor.

It wasn't water. It was paraffin.

Looking back, it is questionable whether the greater idiot was the one who left paraffin lying around in a topless bucket next to a rack of Primuses, or the one who thought that liquid water could remain liquid in an open bucket on the floor of the connecting tunnel.

The first of these was not the met. man. The second one was.

Scared quite witless, he retreated behind the heavy hut door and closed it. Further down the corridor was a rack of blue dry powder extinguishers which only needed to drop on the floor to go off spectacularly.

He knew this because Ian the diesel mechanic, had brushed past these one day while rushing through to the generator shed and pulling on his anorak at the same time. One of the things dropped to the floor and the entire corridor was filled with thick choking white powder. It didn't stop "Ee", who merely muttered some Gaelic imprecations of dubious politeness and swept on. Sweeping was what the rest of the scientific community did for most of the rest of that day.

Grabbing three of the things, he ran back to the door, cautiously opened it to see a raging inferno and, feeling rather like a WW2 comic-book hero, hurled the extinguishers in, one after the other, like grenades. Being a coward at heart, he then shut the door.

Some minutes later, after the hissing had died down, he cautiously opened the door.

It was like Santa's Grotto. Everything was covered in a blanket of fine white, except where the shiny brass of the now dead Primuses gleamed through. Powder, powder everywhere.

There was a certain beauty to the scene—an "after the storm" quality, a sort of volcanic post-coital deathly-pale peace reigned. It was a bloody sight better than the alternative would have been. The met. man went back to the Met. office, poured himself a stiff whisky and after some moments contemplation, picked up a broom and a dustpan and brush.

CHAPTER TWELVE

Eliason Fields.

A mongst the strange and wonderful vehicles cobbled together at Halley by enthusiastic mechanics, some ancient models of commercial snowmobiles and others entirely "sui generis", we had a 1950's "Eliason motor-toboggan" made in the USA.

Motor-toboggans went back a long way. Indeed, there had been at least one on Scott's ill-fated expedition. The early ones were highly unreliable, the motors primitive and underpowered and subject to all kinds of mechanical problems exacerbated by the extreme cold.

The Eliason was a prototype if you like of the now ubiquitous "skidoo"—a highly successful machine, the most modern of which can easily hit 150 kilometres per hour and which have (pure luxury this) electrically heated handlebar grips, so that one's fingers do not get too cold when travelling at speed. Today's models are flashy, with go-faster stripes and styled like an Italian racing car.

The Eliason was none of these things, but oozed charm. I decided to adopt it. The previous year Ken had adopted it and had some success in running it, but the machine had a track which was primitive in comparison with today's ridged rubber belt running over nylon wheels.

The Eliason had two bicycle chains running around large steel cogs, two to each chain. The chains were about one foot apart and were attached transversely by a number of aluminium bars, which provided the contact with the surface and when rotating, pushed the device along, as does the ridged rubber belt in modern skidoos. Apart from the difficulty of adjusting the tension of the chains and keeping them lubricated, the track was open to the elements and also to unwary feet.

Ken, while driving, got a leg caught in the track, was lucky not to have it broken, and after cutting the engine (not an easy thing to do), limped away in great pain and obvious anger. The anger was turned with remarkable efficiency, into constructive work. The workshop echoed with hammering and bending grunting and thumping noises until finally an aluminium shield emerged, which, after some testing and adjustment, was fitted to cover the front part of the track, thus ensuring that no-one could ever again get his leg caught in the device.

The machine was given the nickname of the "Elsan", this being also the name of a proprietary chemical toilet used in the field.

It was largely made of wood, with a seat, wooden runners with the front part of the runners separate from the rear and attached to a steering wheel so that the front runners could be turned.

It was not a very effective steering mechanism, having a turning circle of some 25 metres! The chains with the track runners attached ran over a wooden frame comprising 4 struts, two above and two below. At the back was the motive power, a 4-stroke petrol Briggs and Stratton lawn-mower engine.

The engine was the star of the machine. Not built for speed, after all, not many lawn-mowers go in for racing, it chugged away reliably for ever. Indeed, the problem was stopping it, for once in motion, with a heavy flywheel attached, the spark from the plug appeared to be almost superfluous and after cutting the engine it was an age before the thing actually stopped. This would prove to be something of a disadvantage in the field.

The Elsan was painted in colours somewhat reminiscent of the nursery, the wooden seat, engine-mount and petrol tank were in green, runners and toolbox (thoughtfully attached) in red, steering wheel in black plastic and various other parts in yellow. It would not have looked out of place in a playground for 5 year olds. It was not in good condition. In particular the track was a disaster, having been bodged (repaired in a not entirely professional manner) for years. The track frame, in wood, was practically worn away, particularly the lower part which was rapidly eroded since the full weight of the machine and rider were placed on it as the chains and bars scraped over it.

The engine, good as it was, needed a thorough de-coke of the single cylinder and an equally thorough cleaning of the magneto and the points. The dog-clutch which connected the engine to the tracks when the engine was revved sufficiently was also past its best. In short a total overhaul was required.

Fortunately, a very full set of spares and tools were available, having been kept for over 20 years. A whole winter season was available for the task. The machine was brought into the only partly completed workshop and dismantled, every piece numbered and labelled and sketches made so that the thing could be put back together.

The biggest job was replacement of the track runners and 2" x 2" oak was selected for this. Four lengths were required of perfectly straight oak and this was not possible to find. Part of the oak was twisted slightly. The twisted part was used for the two top runners, since these did not bear the weight of the machine and its driver. The straight oak was required for the two lower runners which took a lot of punishment.

The chains were by far the worst aspect of the machine. Repaired and replaced at various times in the past, they were of slightly unequal length and since the only way of lengthening or shortening them was to insert or remove a half-link and the difference was less than this, they would never be quite right. The chains ran around the two sets of large cogs—two cogs per axle.

The axles, one at each end, should normally be parallel, but to compensate for the slight difference in the length of chain, they could be "shimmed" so as to make them slightly unparallel. This would make the distance between the opposite cogs slightly different and compensate for the difference in length of the chains.

This however, was not easy to do and the result would always be a slightly twisted chain which would suffer considerable wear and tend to come off the cog.

The new oak lower runners were reinforced with Kevlar, used on sledge runners to lessen friction on the snow. In this case, it was to lessen friction on the revolving chains.

The whole chain assembly, about 3 feet long and comprising two large cogs at each end, the two chains and 4 oak runners was fixed at the front end only and free to move vertically at the rear end.

The disadvantage of this was that if the vehicle stuck, increasing the throttle and speeding up the engine would often result in the speeding track simply digging a huge hole in the snow with the rear end disappearing into it. Snow would be hurled into the air and after the engine was killed (which took some time) the entire vehicle would have to be dug out.

Care was therefore exercised with the throttle, but another design fault made the throttle occasionally stick open. The valve on the engine which controlled the flow of fuel was operated by a simple bicycle brake cable from a lever made from 'L'-shaped aluminium attached to the side of the seat. Alas, in order for the cable when pulled, to pull the lever down, the cable needed to point upwards, where the outer plastic sheath was fixed, so that the inner wire cable would pull the lever.

This meant that snow, inevitable thrown up as powder when under way, would settle on the exposed cable end, melt, drip down into the cable sheath and then freeze, thus sticking the cable in place and making it impossible to reduce speed.

This was dangerous for the obvious reason that the Elsan might not stop or slow down as you neared an obstacle or worse still a gaping void and if the Elsan did stop, then the track assembly would dig itself deep into the bundu as described above.

Sophisticated engineering was not a concept with which we were familiar and so the "bodge" adopted was to cover the lever and cable with a polythene bag, held in place by elastic bands

As one might imagine, the tool-kit for the Elsan in some respects resembled more the contents of an old lady's sewing box, than a serious box of mechanic's tools.

After weeks of work in the partially-built workshop, the finished vehicle was unveiled on a sunny and pleasant day. I must say, I was rather proud of it. Not only had the engine been thoroughly cleaned and de-coked, but the piston rings were replaced, the valves cleaned and various worn springs and things replaced and amazingly enough put back together in more or less the correct order.

The new track and renovated chains ran over the brand new oak track guides and to crown it all a new paint job made it look more like something from science fiction than a children's play ground.

The main runners were pillar box red, as was the seat, and the fuel tank. The engine and ancillary parts were painted silver, as was the tool box and the steering wheel and other details were painted black so that it resembled, in colour if not performance, a rather expensive motor-bike.

To say I was proud of it would be an understatement, but others looked distinctly askance at it. After a while, I understood their point of view. The repainting job was the equivalent of putting go-faster stripes and a rear aerodynamic "wing" on a Model T Ford.

CHAPTER THIRTEEN

The Gill.

The Gill was a monster. No-one liked the thing. It stood, or rather lurked, in its own small cubicle in a corner of the balloon shed, a steel galvanised example of what could be said to be a typically British contraption.

On top there was tank with water and added blue anti-freeze. A glass tube gauge indicated how full the tank was. Underneath that was a kind of funnel arrangement with a wide tube to pour one of the two chemical components into. On the other side was another. At the base was a release valve to send the used chemical mixture down into a pit underneath. All around the base was an area of slush which burned skin if touched, being the remains of concentrated caustic soda mixed with snow.

The thing was hated by all who had to use it. It was a relic of the 1950's and had probably worked well at one time, but decades of use and some degree of neglect had left it dilapidated and very much at the end of its useful life.

It was a hydrogen-producing machine, using very basic chemistry, namely the reaction of aluminium powder with caustic soda flakes and water to produce hydrogen — very wet hydrogen at that, to fill the meteorological balloon which was used each day to send a sonde into the atmosphere.

The sonde team was made up of the radar driver and radar plotter, cosily ensconced in the warm radar, the "ditter", cosily ensconced in the met office listening to the Morse code of the sonde as it rose through the atmosphere and decoding the temperature, pressure and humidity — and the balloon launcher, not cosily ensconced at all, but wrestling with the balloon in the depths of the balloon shed, trying to fill it with poor quality wet hydrogen.

It was the balloon launcher who had the worst job by far. He it was who, early in the morning, went out to the balloon shed, some distance away from the comfortable base and descended the precarious ladder to the depths of the deeply buried shed, whose walls and ladders had been raised year after year since 1958.

Down in the cold depths of the place, the Gill had to be fed with its ration of aluminium powder and then caustic soda flakes. These ingredients were then funnelled together with water and the result was an exothermic chemical reaction producing hydrogen and water.

The hydrogen was led through a pipe into the neck of the rubber or neoprene balloon laid out on the floor of the shed, and which gradually filled and rose as the hydrogen dribbled in. Inevitably the balloon launcher got aluminium powder and caustic soda flakes in various parts of his clothing and despite all precautions, such as old over-clothes, gloves with masking tape and goggles, burning caustic dust would always get through and irritate the skin.

As the balloon filled, there was a knack of shaking it in order for the water, entering the balloon with the hydrogen and freezing solid, to shake down to the neck of the balloon and thence out. Water or ice left in the balloon greatly shortened its life as it ascended and in some cases made the balloon burst before it had reached the top of the balloon shed shaft.

The fact that the balloon had to negotiate the shaft was a major disadvantage, which often resulted in damage to the skin of the balloon and a less than satisfactory flight.

This was the situation when the Gill was working well.

By 1974 it usually wasn't and it regularly blocked when the caustic soda flakes and aluminium powder, instead of being fine and dry and reacting properly, became damp and clumped together, preventing a complete reaction and blocking up the Gill completely.

This could cause a build up of hydrogen which was potentially very dangerous and the machine had to be unblocked. This entailed getting down on the freezing ground and using a large pipe wrench to open the drain at the bottom of the machine and in the process getting thoroughly soaked with caustic mixture and freezing water in the burning cesspit beneath the thing, which, because of the mass of heat released into the ice below, leaned at a somewhat precarious angle.

The drain was sealed with a heavy screw-in plug and this was invariably oxidized and frozen. The difficulty of unscrewing it was hard to exaggerate. The main problem was the limited space in which to manoeuvre the large spanner. Why do so-called designers never think of these things?

The spanner gripped a large brass hexagonal plug and frequently slipped, since brass is softer than steel. Why do designers never think of this?

Hitting the end of the spanner with a large hammer to unjam the plug entailed lying underneath the monster, face up with an arm twisted practically out of its socket and the other elbow deep in highly caustic mush. Should the banging finally and unpredictably loosen the plug and the spanner turn a little too far, the plug would drop out under gravity and the weight of the horrible caustic mix above it which would then stream out onto the ground, or onto your face if you didn't get out of the way quickly enough.

Obviously the designer was safe in the knowledge that he would never have to use the damn thing.

The job of filling the balloon thus came to be dreaded and a week of this was the lot of each meteorologist every 4th week. Sunday evening had been one of hard partying and so on Monday morning I made my way wearily and with a monumental hangover up the ladder and out onto the blinding white bundu.

I wore old outer clothing specially selected for the job of operating the Gill. It was caked in caustic soda, full of holes, and wherever skin touched the material, it burned.

The combination of the blinding light, the outrageously loud crunching of the snow crust and the burning sensation from the clothing was nauseous.

It took an age to get over to the balloon shed. The old balloon shed had been there for a long time and the exit shaft had been extended a number of times. This made descent hazardous and also affected the exit of the filled balloon, which easily rubbed against the side of the shaft and was either damaged and thus would burst early before getting high enough into the atmosphere to give a good plot of winds and atmospheric profile.

Worst of all it could burst on the way out of the shaft, which meant filling another balloon, which meant refilling the damn contraption.

Descending into the shed was a hazardous business at the best of times, down a vertical ladder covered with frost. With a violent, nauseous headache it was a thoroughly miserable experience.

The powder released when tipping the caustic flakes into the aperture caused gagging and vomiting given my already delicate condition, but not enough vomiting to relieve the symptoms of extreme nausea.

The addition of the aluminium powder was less nauseous, but the subsequent bending down to floor level to ensure that the hydrogen was emerging was extremely so, as was the smell of the latex balloon when taken from its box. Somehow, in a green daze, I did all that was necessary and the balloon slowly filled with wet hydrogen. Once full, and it seemed an eternity, I shook the neck of the balloon to rid it of ice crystals and tied it off, attaching the radar reflector and the string which led up to the sonde.

Letting the tracker know by the speaker link to the radar, I let the balloon go and it shot up the shaft, hit the side, burst and collapsed in a rubbery heap at the bottom of the shaft.

It was the worst possible outcome. If it had only waited 5 minutes and then burst it would have counted as a balloon flight and that would have been that. As it was, it was an abort and a new balloon had to be filled and that meant going back to the bloody Gill and making some more hydrogen.

There was nothing to be done. Back to the thing I went and fed the caustic flakes and then the aluminium powder into the machine. It blocked and no amount of banging with a wrench would unblock it. The surrounding air being blue by this time I took another whack at the thing, missed the target of the combustion chamber and hit and smashed the coolant water gauge, thus releasing the coolant which soaked away into the snow below.

It was the end. The machine was unusable without the coolant and there were no more replacement parts. It was 4 weeks to relief and the much anticipated arrival of a new hydrogen generator.

In the meantime we were supposed to fly a balloon sonde every day. We had a limited stock of hydrogen in cylinders and worked out that we could do a flight every 3 days using the cylinders until the new hydrogen generator arrived.

We had been promised a new hydrogen generator. No more clunky, primitive nauseous chemical reaction, but a methanol "cracker". This machine would be gleaming, shiny, and electronically controlled. Using barrels of Methanol pumped easily into the reaction tank, high voltage electricity and a platinum catalyst would magically produce dry hydrogen and fill a very large storage tank which would be in the new balloon shed.

Yes, a newly built balloon shed on the surface (at least for a while). This new shed would have storage space for the generator of course, and the new storage tank and space for the radar reflectors used to track the balloon up in the loft. We couldn't wait.

In December, the ship arrived and relief began. Sections of balloon shed were magically erected on the new site. Before the wall sections were closed a cargo sledge brought a rectangular-shaped machine, painted a fetching dark green, with an electronic panel on one end and various switches, valves and chromium plated taps. It looked wonderful. The new storage tank was then installed and linked to the generator with smooth plastic reinforced tubes which fitted together easily with a kind of socket.

No grease was necessary and indeed no grease or oil was possible. We had learnt at an early stage that lubricants of any kind and Hydrogen do not mix except explosively and the brass valves and taps of the bright red hydrogen cylinders were never greased or oiled.

Once the walls were in place, work started on painting the new storage tank bright red for hydrogen. So splendid did the new balloon shed and its installations look that we affixed a nautical clock on a polished mahogany base upon the wall next to the intercom linking the shed with the base.

The electrician came to attach the high voltage cable to the machine and give it a going over, removing all the plastic packaging to reveal the thing in all its glory. Methanol was pumped into the reaction tank—a clean hygienic process with no resemblance at all to the awful messy chemical fuelling of the old Gill.

Never had we looked forward to anything quite as much as this in the world of Antarctic meteorology.

The time came to switch the machine on and fill the hydrogen tank with a whole week's worth of gas. From then, just a stroll in the morning, then up the outside ladder, down the inside ladder and take out a balloon attach it to the nozzle and turn on the tap to fill it with clean, dry hydrogen. We had dreams of balloons going higher into the stratosphere than they ever had before, since there would be no ice in the balloon to cause it to burst.

Champagne was brought to the shed and glasses set out for the official turning on. The electrician was there, the Base Commander, the head geophysicist from the UK and the met team for the great event.

After final checking the machine was switched on. A hum ensued, but otherwise nothing seemed to be happening. High voltage "cracking methanol" into its component parts including hydrogen was a quiet, civilized, unpretentious affair. The pressure gauge on the tank was watched assiduously as it would indicate the filling of the tank up to the maximum pressure. Naturally, this would take time, such was the size of the tank.

After three-quarters of an hour, no reading appeared on the gauge. This was not surprising we were told. The tank would have to contain quite a considerable amount of hydrogen before the pressure would register at all. Just in case, a quick check was made of the connections to ensure that there were no leaks.

Time passed. Someone suggested we open the bottle of champagne anyway before it froze and this suggestion was taken up enthusiastically. A selection of cheesy things was passed around and everyone congratulated everyone else. Otherwise all eyes were on the machine, which continued to hum, but otherwise seemed quite impassive.

Half an hour later there was still no sign of any pressure in the storage tank. Well, you know, it is such a big tank, said the Chief Geophysicist. These things take time to fill up. Of course, once it is filled up, you can just top up the pressure every day or so and the tank will be always full or nearly so.

In case of problems with the balloon or other problems, you could easily fill 3 or 4 balloons in one morning should the need arise.

There was no heating in the shed and in another half an hour we were becoming a little chilly. The champagne was all gone and what remained in a few glasses was as flat as our spirits were becoming. The head Geo decided to take a closer look and detached the connecting tube to the tank and put his finger over the end. The pressure should be discernible on his finger after a few moments.

Funnily enough, it wasn't. It was at this point that the electrician decided to switch the thing off and do something with the wiring, after consulting the large book of instructions which came with the machine.

Having accomplished this, he reconnected the tube to the tank. "Looks like the wiring was wrongly installed" he said optimistically. We waited longer. Feet got cold despite mukluks and the encouraging comments heard previously became distinctly muted. Nothing changed on the pressure gauge.

Various people drifted away to get warm. The remainder stared hard at the pressure gauge almost willing the pointer to move. "Perhaps it's stuck" said the electrician and gave it a sharp tap with a spanner. Nothing happened.

It began to become obvious that the bloody thing wasn't working and none of us had any idea why. The manuals were consulted, circuit diagrams spread out on the floor and examined in detail. Wagging of heads and scratching of hair was followed by total puzzlement and silence.

Finally someone snapped. A burst of hysterical laughter clove the oppressive silence. It was followed by another, and another and finally the Chief Geo from the UK, who was Scottish and not normally given to humorous outbursts of any kind, found himself also in hysterics.

"They've sent us a bloody machine that doesn't work!" he roared. "The damn thing doesn't do anything!"

Indeed, it did not. Despite repeated attempts over weeks by the electrician to examine its innards, re-wire constituent parts, scrutinise the circuit diagrams with infinite care, the machine refused to do what it was supposed to, namely produce hydrogen.

Relief having ended there was no way spare parts could be obtained even had we known what spare parts, if any, were required. Another barrel of Methanol was tried, in case the first had somehow been contaminated, or even filled with something else. Nothing we did could persuade the thing to work.

For a whole year, balloon flights were strictly rationed to what could be done using hydrogen from cylinders that we had. I believe that the following year the machine was either replaced or repaired and produced what it was supposed to, but by then I had gone home.

A few years later, in an incident which was never satisfactorily explained, the new balloon-shed burned down one night, leading to spectacular fireworks.

The epilogue to all this is that these days, there is no balloon shed, nor is there a hydrogen generator. Today's meteorologists (who include young ladies) simply walk over to the serried ranks of Helium cylinders brought each year by the ship and attach a balloon to the tube and turn on the tap. The balloon fills with dry, non-flammable helium, whose only risk (if inhaled by the filler) is making his or her voice sound like that of Mickey Mouse—(the original designer of both the Gill and the methanol hydrogen generator!)

CHAPTER FOURTEEN

Port and Cigars.

The 1973 relief took place at 2nd Chip, close to Halley and was expedited pretty quickly and with little fuss, unlike the 1974 relief, which had to be done from the Low Shelf.

The usual things occurred. At one point the *Bransfield* was hit by a section of falling ice-cliff, which deposited a large amount of snow and ice on the deck. The weight and impact bent the rail over quite substantially and it had to be heated and bent back again using welding gear.

A small selection of viruses made it to the base occasioning a few sniffles for a few days until the cold killed them off.

The leaving Fids moved from base to ship and the arriving Fids moved the other way. We had a rough 50/50 changeover, including a new BC.

Undoubtedly the most significant aspect of this relief was that there was, of all things, a woman on board ship. The Captain had recently married and his new wife accompanied him on the journey from Southampton.

It was quite a journey. First of all we crossed the North Atlantic in November to the USA. This may seem, indeed is, a strange way to get to Antarctica, but we had been asked by the US to pick up some cargo for their base at Palmer Station from the Sea-Bee base in Provincetown, Rhode Island. For us this meant a few days in New England, but not before a considerable fright.

Just short of the US coast we encountered a hurricane force depression with winds at Force 11 and huge seas. We went backwards for 3 days and foolhardy souls went up to the bridge and out onto the bridge deck where you could hang on the radio aerial (crossed steel circles) by your arms and have the sensation of being sandblasted by rain and hail.

Many were sick and bunk-ridden and so the Fiddery was deserted. This was just as well, for a steel beer barrel broke loose and careened from side to side of the Fiddery as the Bransfield rolled furiously. The barrel hardly touched the floor, but it did touch the Parker Knoll lounge chairs considerably, to the extent that they were smashed into a collection of matchwood. No one dared go in. It would have been suicide and all we could do was watch the destruction helplessly from the reinforced window in the closed door.

The waves had been estimated at 50 feet high and the danger was of the ship, which being an icebreaker was not configured for high seas, broaching to and taking a huge roll. For this reason one night the Captain called for the second main engine to be started to provide more power to prevent a broach. Alas the second engine was not started in time due to the indisposition of the Chief Engineer. For this "indisposition" he was relieved of his job the moment we arrived in the USA.

In the meantime the ship broached to and took a monumental 55-degree roll. The damage in the ship was considerable. In cabins, people fell out of bunks and stereo equipment and other personal items were hurled from one wall to the other and back. We were lucky that the Bransfield was as seaworthy as she was. She could have rolled and not recovered and had that happened, this would not be written.

After our stay in the USA, we sailed along the coast of the USA and into the Caribbean. Here we dawdled somewhat, to our delight and spent wonderful days in the sun admiring the islands we passed and the unforgettable sunsets. We had no doubt who to thank for this unexpected cruise—the Captain of course, but more precisely his new wife. She may have felt that after the North Atlantic, she deserved something more relaxing and we all benefited.

We continued down the coast of South America, spending days passing through the muddy and fresh water sent out far into the ocean by the Amazon, watching the lights of fires in small fishing boats at night far out from the coast of Recife.

The Captain's new wife was a civilizing influence on a ship full of Fids and even a moderating influence on the Captain, of whom Fids lived in fear, especially at his inspections on Saturday mornings, where he was notorious for his strictness. Even this seemed to be moderated somewhat and we had no doubt that his new wife had something to do with it.

Relief came and went and it was, as ever, with some relief on the part of the winterers and indeed of some of the new arrivals on base that they looked forward to the Bransfield's departure—"It's not that we don't like you, but we feel it's time for you to go..." pretty much summed up the view of many of us.

We had certainly enjoyed the visit to the base by the Captain's new wife—the very first visit by a female human to Halley. The human must be emphasised since female dogs and indeed a female cat had already accomplished that feat for their own species.

It was late, very late, at night when for some unremembered reason I had to return to the ship from the base on the last night before departure. That day some of us had visited the ship during the evening for the showing of a film. This was an event, since the stock of films on base for the following year was distinctly limited both in quantity and quality. On base we got what appeared to be rejects from the merchant marine film circuit. Whatever their origin, they were uniquely awful "B" grade movies, some of which were so awful that they inadvertently backed into genius.

A classic of the genre was the Australian film "Cattlemen." This film was about taking a road-train full of cattle across the most boring stretch of nothing outside of Antarctica, namely the great Nullabor Plain.

It was enlivened, if that is the right word, by a musical sound track with songs by an Australian yodelling cowboy by the name of Frank Ifield—a favourite, I remember, of my mother.

So bad were the plot and the dialogue that it became a base favourite and was sometimes shown with the sound turned off, the audience providing the soundtrack (which we had come to know by heart).

The chance to see a real "first-rate" movie, as shown to public audiences in cinemas was therefore not to be missed.

Unfortunately the movie on offer on board was a miserable affair called: "They shoot horses, don't they?" This deadly dull and depressing offering was about people dancing marathons for money during the Great Depression in the USA. As a send-off for those about to spend a year in Antarctic isolation it was about as motivational as a Leonard Cohen album.

Thus, when I returned to the ship at getting on for 11 p.m. it was after having watched this dismal epic during the early evening.

I took one of the base skidoos and drove on a fine evening along the line of oil-drums to 2nd Chip. The position of the ship against the cliff made it possible to walk out onto the ice-cliff with little difficulty and as I parked the skidoo carefully pointing inland, I admired the pink and grey "sundown"- not "sunset", since at this time of year sunset didn't happen. It was, in fact, the midnight sun.

Parking the skidoo pointing inland was a reflexive action already after only one week on base.

Only a day into relief a brand new skidoo had been unloaded onto the ice-cliff, all shiny and beautiful in its wooden crate.

The crate having been opened, the wood removed and the plastic unwrapped from the gleaming machine, it stood, mean and fast looking, in bright yellow, shiny black and silver.

It was fuelled with 2 -stroke mix (40:1 petrol to oil at Halley instead of the usual 20:1, to prevent the spark-plug oiling up in the low temperatures).

The tractor mechanic, with great ceremony, stood next to the machine and prepared to start it using the starter-cord, the black plastic handle of which had to be pulled quickly and cleanly to turn the engine over and start the cycle.

The engine was connected to the tracks by a dog clutch, governed by the speed of the engine. Once you accelerated the engine to a certain speed, the clutch engaged and you were off. In this case, all too literally.

The skidoo, once the case was removed, was pointed towards the edge of the ice-cliff, but was not so close to it as to pose a problem. Once the engine started and the driver was seated on it, it could easily be turned around and driven inland to the base.

What had not been realised, most unfortunately, was that the accelerator cable was stuck.

As a result, when the starter cord was pulled, the engine revved furiously, the clutch immediately engaged and without waiting for the driver, the skidoo shot forwards and over the edge of the ice-cliff.

It was a good thing it didn't have the driver sitting on it, since it unapologetically sank without trace in 500 metres of very cold water.

Having watched all this with great interest, the need to park a skidoo facing inland was engraved upon my memory. At least if the thing shot off on its own, it would head off across the snow and one might just manage to run after it, or at least see where it was headed and go look for it when it ran out of fuel.

I had a camera with me, a new Pentax SLR bought from Eric, the Chief Steward. It had black and white film in it for reasons, which are no longer clear to me, but may have had something to do with the idea that black and white photography was somehow considered to be more artistic.

As I got off the skidoo, I saw a group of officers emerging, complete with port and cigars and dressed in formal attire, for an after-dinner walk on the ice-cliff to admire the view. Stuart, the First Officer, was there, as was Eric, who had sold me my camera. The captain was also there as was,- glory be,- his delightfully-attired wife.

In the foreground were a number of inquisitive Adelie penguins, which do not winter at Halley—only the Emperor penguin does that.

The Adelie is much smaller and looks very similar to a manager from the Co-op at the annual dinner dance—portly, slightly comic and full of self-importance.

Graham Chambers

This penguin is usually found in lower latitudes, along the Antarctic peninsular, and very close to what we at Halley tended to call the "banana belt" It was named by the Belgian explorer Adrien de Gerlache, who named the penguins, for reasons perhaps best left unresearched, after his wife.

Thus it was that the picture was taken of a group of officers and gentlemen and their female companion in the company of similarly attired local fauna.

Every time I ever showed this photo subsequently, I was congratulated on the almost undetectable darkroom superposition of penguins on a photo of people in evening dress or the almost undetectable darkroom superposition of people in evening dress on a photo of penguins.

CHAPTER FIFTEEN

Dear John.

A curious, but never mentioned, aspect of life on base at that time was the complete physical absence of women.

There were plenty of representations of women. At one point a full size cardboard cut-out of an Air Stewardess for some incomprehensible reason inhabited one of the workshops. Up in the lofts, a vast store of pages containing pictures of naked ladies was to be found, evidently much thumbed.

We had no internet, no satellite TV and even if we had had these things, despite the supposed licentiousness of the 1960's, there simply were no TV channels devoted to naked ladies in those days. So "Playboy" and similar publications was all we had.

These days, with females on base, perhaps political correctness (which also did not exist in our day) has ensured that any sort of representation of a naked lady is banned.

Apart from that aspect of the matter, one cannot really say that women, per se, were missed. Particular females certainly were missed, by their particular boyfriends, and in very few cases, husbands. We were a young lot and not many were married or even contemplating it at the time. One or two may have been divorced, some may have come to Antarctica to escape the female gender in a similar way to those who join the French Foreign Legion. People in that situation rarely talked about it.

The idea that it would have been nice to have some females to cook, clean and wash clothes of course is now deeply incorrect and possibly would have been seen as offensive even then. Still there is no doubt that some of these activities could perhaps have been done better by females, though even this, in these days, is not certain.

Some females had applied to the British Antarctic Survey and there were some who were perfectly well qualified in science and also in expedition skills, but the BAS shied away from taking the ultimate step, using all sorts of arguments to deter what was by the 1970s already seen as inevitable. There would have to be two sets of toilet and bathroom facilities—an obvious disadvantage where resources, building materials and manpower were at a premium.

There would be terrible jealousies and hatreds and possible violence between the males. This particular fear probably arose from what may have been an apocryphal situation on a US base in the 1950s where there was one female among 20 odd men and she was the wife of the base leader. She is reputed to have become pregnant and the base leader was not responsible. (How anyone knew this was never explained!) A fight had broken out, the base carbines had been taken from the locker, shots exchanged and wounds received in consequence

There were probably some hard-core veterans who simply did not want the unsullied environment of the Antarctic to be invaded by women. What about their damned accessories, vanity-cases, cosmetics, umpteen changes of clothes. What about the monthly curse? Think of the consequences for base morale!

What about field work, with two people sharing a tent! If one was female, the consequences could be appalling!

Some of the reasons advanced as to why having females in the Antarctic was impossible, unthinkable and so on stretched logic and common-sense to breaking point and either assumed that the females would be so attractive and so hungry for male company that "the inevitable would occur", or that the males were so desperate, so testosterone-fuelled and so immature that "the inevitable would occur."

This sort of thinking was undignified and demeaning to both men and women. Nonetheless, even when, led by stalwart politicians such as Barbara Castle, the political wind was swinging in favour of equal rights, equal pay and equality generally for women, BAS hid behind the façade that it was actually a Falkland Islands outfit rather than a UK mainland one and therefore the somewhat less liberated views and customs of the colonial Falklands applied.

Of course in the 1980's all of this was swept away and the full admission of women into all and any of the British Antarctic Survey's posts rapidly became inevitable with improved technology helping considerably with the building and logistical requirements.

But this was all to come. In the meantime couples, married or otherwise, could keep in touch by means of a telex of 50 words a month from home to the base and 25 words from the base to home.

The youth of most of us meant that the 25 words had sometimes to be divided between parents and girlfriends. You couldn't say a lot in twelve words, so usually it was 25 to the girlfriend one month and 25 to the parents the next.

The difference in word allowance -50 words to us but only 25 from us -was dictated by the telex capacity of the base and the priority accorded to other traffic, basically science results and logistics communications. In fact, it helped to have only 25 words since, being male, many of us were not exactly loquacious, some indeed verged on the taciturn, and any more than that would have entailed serious effort on the part of some of us to find anything to add.

Our journey to Halley Bay took us first of all to the other BAS bases in Antarctica (a privilege for Halley winterers since Halley Bay was the most remote base and closest to the South Pole).

Thus, after leaving the Falkland Islands, we got to see the base at South Georgia, a satellite base at Bird Island off South Georgia, Signy Island (a base principally for biologists), then Argentine Island (beautifully situated near the Lemaire Channel on the Antarctic peninsular, which runs up like a finger pointing to South America) and finally Adelaide Island at the base of the Antarctic Peninsular which had an airstrip and was quite busy with flights taking geologists and glaciologists to remote camps.

Finally we were able to visit the much-fabled Stonington, where great deeds of dog sledging had been carried out in more romantic times.

At most of these bases, there was, on the bar, a book of "Dear Johns". These, of course, were letters received by men on base from their girlfriends (possibly wives!) from home and which were not perhaps so intimate as they once had been (i.e. the year before).

With such limitations on telex messages and of course, to repeat, no internet, the arrival of the ship for the annual relief was awaited with much anticipation not only for the food and drink and fuel which it brought, but perhaps above all for the mail.

At Halley it was the custom for the Bransfield (our supply ship) to head directly to a lower part of the ice-shelf near the intended berthing point and ram the ice front so that the bow of the ship was in contact with the ice.

At this point a crew member emerged with one or more sacks of mail. Dressed often in sledging red, he looked for all the world like Father Christmas and he would make his way to the bow and hand over or drop down (depending on the height of the ice-front at that point) the sacks of mail. The excitement that this aroused is hard to imagine today, but the sacks would be put onto a skidoo, which then shot off at speed towards the base.

Once inside, the sacks would be emptied onto the floor of the bar and the contents distributed (by the shouting of names) to the eager recipients. Naturally the number, nature and smell of the mail handed out would occasion great comment, often ribald.

Some missives would be heavily drenched in perfume, some would be heavily drenched in disappointment (usually these would be buff envelopes of an official-looking kind) and large parcels would be looked at enviously with anticipation of possibly shared "goodies".

Sometimes over-eager recipients of obviously personal letters would enthusiastically (and foolishly) open the letter right there in front of everyone else in the base bar, which was where the mailbag usually ended up. In many cases a sudden swoop by a by-standing colleague would whisk the missive out of the recipient's hands and gallop around the room reading from the letter whilst hotly pursued by the victim of the theft, whose face would become redder and redder from the exertion of the chase plus the excruciating embarrassment occasioned by the content. Others would impede the chase while guffaws rent the air as the more salacious bits of the letter were digested.

Most of us were young and unmarried. The overall youth of the base complement had thoroughly mystified the Russians of the 23rd Soviet Antarctic expedition when they visited Halley Bay and, in a version of cartoon aliens landing on planet Earth asked to be "taken to our leader". Their puzzlement on discovering that the "leader" was, in their eyes, a callow youth who had only just started shaving was palpable.

Had we been a complement of men married for some time then no doubt the reaction of our wives, on hearing that their husband was off to Antarctica for a few years, would have been one of relief to get the old bugger from under her feet. Alas, our relationships were usually of fairly recent vintage and thus young and tender hothouse plants which had not had time to put down much in the way of tap-roots.

As a result, many did not survive and the evidence of this was in the number of letters in which it was obvious that passion had cooled, and not just because of the ambient temperatures experienced during the voyage. Although tragic (momentarily at least) for the recipient, the letters concerned were often unintentionally extremely funny.

A classic was the admission, by the young lady, that "she had found another", by the name of Roger (it is not recorded whether he was a lodger) and was sure that "if you were to meet Roger, I am sure you would find him as wonderful a person as I do." (-this addressed to the (former) boyfriend, who no doubt, had he met the eponymous Roger, would have shaken him warmly by the throat).

Graham Chambers

The ultimate destination for many of these missives was the scrapbook kept on the base bar. Often the letters were accompanied by a photograph of the sender.

In one particular case, perhaps on Adelaide Island, the photograph was not so easy to see in detail since it was perforated with rather large holes, each one with a burn mark round the edge. On receipt of the letter, the recipient had signed the base firearms book, taken the base .303 rifle and some ammunition and, setting up the photograph on a suitable pole some distance away, had fired away with, presumably, fury and remarkably enough, extreme precision at the image of the former beloved.

CHAPTER SIXTEEN

Gloria a O'Higgins.

Our journey south was rather more touristy than most Fids managed. The reason for this was the presence aboard the Bransfield of the Captain's new wife. It was in the way of a honeymoon for them and therefore, after crossing the North Atlantic in November (not a fun experience) to pick up cargo in Rhode Island, we sailed lazily down the coast of the USA, stopping in Chesapeake Bay to pick up more cargo.

Thereafter, instead of sailing directly south we diverted somewhat into the Caribbean and while chipping and painting on deck were delighted by flying fish, dolphins and passing volcanic islands—all the while luxuriating in the sunshine and tropical temperatures.

Following a course parallel to the coast of Brazil we sailed for days in brownish water, which I was told was largely fresh and was the outpouring from the Amazon, whose mouth at this point was 200 miles wide. Continuing along the coast to Uruguay, we sailed into another estuary, that of the River Plate (or Rio de La Plata) where just offshore from Montevideo could still be seen the mast of the German pocket battleship "Graf Spee", scuttled by her captain in 1942 after being trapped by a British naval squadron.

Before heading into Antarctic waters proper, we sailed around Cape Horn, which, despite its fearful reputation, was as calm as a millpond. From there we were headed to the Chilean port of Punta Arenas in the province of Magellanes. To do this, we had to sail west along the channel separating Tierra del Fuego from the mainland.

A hazard of this operation was that the strait separated Argentina and Chile and these two neighbours were not friendly, having quarrelled over the dividing line between them in precisely this area. We were approached from the Argentinian port of Rio Gallegos by a rather down-at-heel pilot cutter (to be gracious about the description). It was light blue in colour, had seen better days and looked more like an old fishing boat than anything official.

It approached the starboard side of the Bransfield and the Argentinian pilot demanded to board as our ship was in Argentine waters and must be piloted through the channel. With some reluctance on the part of our Captain the cutter came alongside and the heavily-set and moustachioed pilot, looking the part in heavy sunglasses, heaved himself aboard and after strained introductions, insisted on lodging himself on the starboard bridge wing—an external balcony.

No sooner had he settled on the bridge wing when a low, sleek and very dangerous-looking motor torpedo boat appeared off the port bow. It was a Chilean navy MTB with a very efficient-looking gun mounted for'ard of the cabin. It determinedly bore down on the Bransfield and radio contact told us that it was carrying a Chilean pilot, who insisted that we were in Chilean waters and therefore must be guided by a Chilean pilot.

Having little choice in the matter, the Captain allowed the MTB alongside and a very smart Chilean officer in white gloves saluted and demanded to be installed on the bridge.

The situation was farcical. The Argentine pilot looked daggers at his Chilean counterpart. The Chilean ignored the scruffy Argentinian and our captain was placed in the unenviable position of navigating diplomatically between two pilots, one on each bridge wing, each of whom had different ideas about the precise route the ship should take. With the Chilean MTB hovering ominously in the background to port and the Argentine hulk staying well and safely astern to starboard, the situation could have turned nasty. However the scruffy Argentine obviously decided that discretion was the better part, and after some hurried radio communication came to the conclusion that we were leaving his country's waters and that he could therefore take his leave of us. He did this with rapid correctness and disappeared from the bridge and rejoined the hulk, which had in the meantime, come up on the starboard side.

Not long after, the Chilean had obviously decided that we needed no further guidance, since the shark-like MTB with a spurt of impressive speed, came up on the port side and with a perfunctory salute, he left and sped off toward the Chilean coast.

In waters such as these navigation demanded diplomacy as well as seamanship.

Anchoring in the Beagle Channel where nearly a century before, Charles Darwin had sailed aboard the "Beagle", we spent New Year's Eve. The surroundings were spectacular, comprising distant snow covered volcanic peaks and long fjords snaking off toward the horizon. The midnight hour and the New Year were preceded by much jollity liberally lubricated from the ship's bar and at midnight Verey lights (normally used as a distress signal), were set off as a substitute for fireworks and the ship's hooters worked overtime.

It was a weary and hung-over ship's company which watched with some pride, the ship's berthing in the Chilean port of Punta Arenas (Sandy Point). The Bransfield being an ice ship, she was fitted with bow thrusters, which made her highly manoeuvrable. She was thus able to insert herself neatly between two other moored ships, with about the same facility as a neatly parked car, causing crew on the other ships and observers on the quay to break into spontaneous applause.

Before arrival in Chile, we all had to fill out a customs form which contained the most curious questions and regulations. Among the things we were not allowed to bring into Chile were matches (a state monopoly), parrots (perhaps an agricultural hazard) and theodolites (which puzzles me still).

It had only been a couple of months ago that the President of Chile Salvador Allende, had been forcibly ousted in a military coup (the first and only coup in Chile's history) led by a, then unknown, soldier by the name of Pinochet.

Once further formalities were accomplished we were allowed ashore. Military security was very tight and our impression made scarier by the fact that Chilean troops wore very similar uniforms to the German army in WW2, indeed with identical helmets. In addition, when the soldiers marched in a company, they used a form of goose-step, making the impression even more chilling.

Punta Arenas was a town of grid-iron streets, laid over a series of small steep hills and thus the streets in some directions were very steep indeed. There were a few high rise buildings, but mostly single storey blocks. There were two particularly noticeable features. It was remarkably quiet with very few people out on the streets, and the shops were practically denuded of goods. Shop window after shop window was virtually empty. Butcher's shops had no meat and perhaps a couple of cans of corned beef were all they had on display. It was clear that before the military coup, there had been economic meltdown.

The feature of the town that amused us most was the prominence of the name "O'Higgins". There was a "Banco O'Higgins", an "Avenida O'Higgins" and a "Plaza O'Higgins".

A trip arranged with a local tourist firm in a minibus to a cape a little to the south where whales could be seen spouting in the bay, was accompanied by a visit to a small museum made of very weathered wood of silver hue. Inside were artefacts from the 19th century including a beautifully worked blue silken banner, exquisitely embroidered with scenes from Chilean history and the wonderfully wrought (in silver and gold thread) motto: "Gloria a O'Higgins"! It struck me then as ludicrous and over thirty years later, it still does.

Back in town a square was graced with a statue of the man himself, pointing with outstretched arm to the Antarctic (Punta Arenas can claim to be the most southerly town in the world) as if to claim it for Chile.

It was not his fault if he was the issue of a Chilean mother and an Irish father. He led the movement for Chilean independence from Spain, helped considerably by the British navy and has therefore become the Chilean national hero, much in the same way as General San Martin became in Argentina. At least the name San Martin sounds congruous in a Spanish speaking country in a way that "O'Higgins" alas, does not.

In the evening a group of us decided to hit the town—not that the nightlife looked very promising. For a start, there was a strict military curfew. We had seen squads of troops going from place to place, but in our youth and relative innocence did not give it much thought. It was only years later when the realization came that these troops were rounding up known left-wingers and supporters of the ousted President for execution or simply disappearance.

Our first bar was a disappointment. The only drinks on offer were Pisco (a kind of South American brandy) drunk with very sour lemon or lime juice and what was termed on the blackboard a "Bladdy Merry", presumably vodka and tomato juice, but no one tried it. We met up with some locals, who seemed agitated and scared but friendly and who invited us to join them in a private celebration of some kind. We followed them into a building and into a large-ish hall full of people and full of food which was pressed upon us together with wine. Such generosity we thought should not go unrewarded and so two of us went quickly back to the ship and brought a couple of bottles of good malt whisky, hidden under our anoraks.

The production of these at the party led to uproar. Hugs and kisses (from both men and women) and much jollity ensued but the whisky disappeared. It was later when we discovered that what had cost us 60p a bottle aboard ship was worth a few month's salary in Punta Arenas at that time.

The reason for the celebration was uncertain, and our Spanish was almost non-existent, but it seemed to revolve around the fact that some of the people present were leaving Punta and possibly even Chile. Again, the sinister aspect of this only became clear years afterwards.

Staggering out into the street as the celebration ended we found ourselves hungry, despite the finger food at the fiesta and we chanced upon an open restaurant. It did not look particularly inviting, but a hungry man will eat almost anything. It tuned out that there was an extremely limited menu. The first course was, according to our small Spanish dictionary "hedgehog". There was no alternative first course and, assured that it was delicious, it duly arrived.

Each of was confronted with a round object smelling of seaweed and ammonia, which when cut open released a semi-liquid gloopy sort of red mess. It tasted repulsive but, not wishing to offend our hosts, someone produced a small plastic bag into which the contents were surreptitiously poured, underneath the table, to be taken away afterwards and dumped.

The second course was a single pork chop- a small pork chop, apparently from a pig suffering from dwarfism and quite possibly a host of other serious veterinary complications.

It was accompanied by a wilted piece of lettuce and two small carrots. We chewed for a long time on the small amount of meat that could be separated from the bone. There was no dessert, so quite a lot of cheap red wine was drunk.

We staggered out of the restaurant rather late, although the sky was still light, as it is in such high latitudes. One of us realized that it was long past the curfew of 10 p.m. so we started back to the ship down one of Punta's very steep streets.

We had hardly gone 10 yards when a military jeep screeched around the corner from behind and above us and came to a halt on the slope next to the kerb where we were standing. All three soldiers, including the driver, jumped out with machine guns pointed at us. We put up our hands and backed off against the wall.

The following seconds seemed to last for an eternity as one of the soldiers barked out orders or questions which we could not understand. There was a kind of stand-off in which the soldiers kept their guns pointed at us and we (scared witless) just stood and stared at their jeep. The reason for our interest was that the jeep (whose handbrake was evidently very poor) was starting to move downhill at an increasingly rapid rate.

Our staring at the jeep started to produce a reaction in the soldiers whose concentration on us wavered somewhat until one of them shot a glance backward at the jeep, which by then was freewheeling downhill. In a matter of excruciating seconds (for us) the soldiers all turned and ran hell for leather downhill after the jeep.

We watched them catch up and one of them jumped in and brought the jeep to a standstill at which point the others jumped in. Waiting in something approaching terror for them to drive back up the hill to their unfinished business with us, we were astonished to see them gun the accelerator and shoot off around the corner, never to be seen by us again.

We scooted back to the ship, relieved and eternally grateful for Latin-American pride and the military's horror of losing face.

Review Requested:
If you loved this book, would you please provide a review at Amazon.com?